Success With Citrus

BY

PATRICIA OLIVER

This book is dedicated to

Jeronimo Santana-Martin

whose hard work and effort at the Citrus Nursery makes everything possible. Without him I would not have had the pleasure of growing citrus and this book would not have been written.

Published by
GLOBAL ORANGE GROVES UK
P.O.BOX 644, POOLE, DORSET, BH17 9YB
Tel 0202 691699

ISBN 0 9522496 O X

Printed in Great Britain
by the Bath Press, Avon.

CONTENTS

ACKNOWLEDGEMENTS

I would like to express my sincere and heartfelt thanks to Joy Davis whose encouragement and assistance enabled me to complete this project.

I would also like to express my thanks to the following people who have all made essential contributions which have been much appreciated.

Allison Gibbs and Malcolm Carwardine who gave their time and expertise in developing recipes and preparing them for the photographer.

Vincent Gibbs who produced the photographs for 'Cooking with Citrus'.

Dr Ralph Vadas BA.MBBS.LRCP.MRCS.MD(USA) G P. for his article on Vitamin C.

Carrie Creswell for the information on Biological Pest Control.

Graeme Grant-Willis, Tony Benham, Richard Stevens, Jonathan Garratt, Nestlés UK Ltd, Cosmetics to Go, and Pronatur, for their contributions.

Special thanks must go to the National Trust who have supplied so much information and many photographs of their Orangeries and also to all the Owners, Trustees, Local Authorities and Archivists who tend and care for the Heritage of our Stately Homes, for their kind permission to write about their Orangeries and reproduce their photographs.

My thanks to Generalidad Valenciana I.V.I.A. for information on the varieties of citrus fruits and the photographs supplied.

COPYRIGHT

 Text Patricia Oliver 1993.

ABOUT THE BOOK

In 1987 we had a large conservatory built along the south wall of our house. We decided we wanted to grow unusual plants that would not normally grow in the English climate. Jeronimo being Spanish, decided that citrus would give us variety, interest and harvest, something for all seasons and never a dull moment.

Information in England about the care of citrus was almost impossible to come by. Presumably because citrus was so scarce, no-one had produced proper growing instructions for them. It was rather trial and error at first, but gradually we got around to studying the Spanish books on citrus, made adaptations because of climatic differences and because the trees were being grown in containers and not planted in fields, and feel confident that the instructions we have outlined in this book and have been issuing with our trees and fertilizer, are the most comprehensive you will find in the UK.

One remark that kept coming up in the early years was that "you could not grow oranges in England". When we advertised our trees, we were told "you are ahead of your time". We have had to educate the public into realising that citrus trees have been grown in England at least since the reign of Elizabeth I and possibly before, and many fine Orangeries still exist to-day to prove this. We have given a brief description of some of these which can be visited to-day. Many have had a change of use, but some still house citrus trees. We have not included Orangeries which are in private use and not open to the public and there may be others which are open but which have not come to our notice.

Interestingly, many Orangeries that may have fallen into disrepair, or had a change of use are now being restored to their former glory and are again being used for the purpose for which they were intended.

The Orangeries were generally built facing south or south-east, with many tall windows designed to catch the light and warmth from the rays of the winter sun. The height of the windows should bear some relationship to the depth of the Orangery, so that light from the the low winter sun will reflect right to the back, maximising the available light. The back of the Orangery itself did not normally contain windows, only a large door.

Winter heat was generally provided by fires or stoves and later with hot water pipes either running around the interior of the Orangery or as underfloor heating. Some records show the trees had a height of 13 feet and a width of 12 feet, but a height of 20 feet has also been recorded. They were all grown in pots or wooden tubs. The doors had to be of a suitable height to allow access for the trees when they were moved outside in the summer. The Orangeries had tiled or slated roofs, not glass.

Orange trees have dark green glossy leaves all year round and in winter and early spring they have white waxen flowers that have a very strong perfume. Some find it exquisite, some find it overpowering, but it is considered to be sweet scented.

The harvest of citrus fruits is generally between October and March, so the orangeries were a pleasant place to walk in the winter, the colour of the fruits in stark contrast to the leaves. With blossom produced often before Easter and while the trees are still inside the Orangery, the fruits and the perfume of the blossom made this the best time for the enjoyment of citrus trees.

The modern conservatory makes an excellent orangery for the winter care of citrus. Even if you can only house one tree, the pleasure and reward from your chosen variety will make it well worthwhile.

Many of the varieties of citrus available to-day are hybrids, specially produced to improve the flavour, the texture and the consumer appeal of the fruits. The consumer also prefers seedless fruits so many of the old seedier varieties are no longer planted. The newer varieties have larger crops, are more reliable, have fewer or no seeds and are less prone to disease. There are photographs and descriptions of many of the more popular varieties of citrus obtainable in Europe to-day to help you to distinguish between them, become more aware of what to look for and to help you choose what to buy, whether it be the fruit from the shops, or the trees to grow your own citrus fruit.

We have gone into detail on how to look after your trees giving help and advice about choosing your pot, the compost to use, watering, feeding, pruning, temperature, ventilation, humidity, pollination and fruiting, the problems you may have and the solutions to those problems. We have developed our own fertilizers specifically for container grown citrus trees, which caters for their special needs. 'Summer Food for Citrus Trees' and 'Winter Food for Citrus Trees', will enable you to get the very best from your trees.

Our research has shown that all parts of the tree, the leaves, the flowers, the nectar and pollen, the fruit peel, the flesh and the juice, have a part to play, not just in the diet, but in health and beauty products, in perfume, in aromatherapy and even in industry. Citrus is a very important plant.

In Britain our use of citrus in cooking has up to now been rather modest, so I have brought together some traditional and new recipes to broaden our use of citrus so that having grown your own fruit, you will find good use for them. Picking citrus fruits fresh from the tree may be a new experience, but one that is certainly enjoyable.

Famous Orangeries To Visit

Oranges by A Mensaque (1863) Found from Anglesey Abbey
National Trust Photographic Library / Derrick E Witty

THE ORANGERY

Attingham Park, Near Shrewsbury, Shropshire, SY4 4TP

The house at Attingham Park was designed in 1785 by George Steuart for the 1st Lord Berwick. It boasts an elegant classical interior decoration and a famous painted boudoir.

The park landscape was designed by Humphry Repton in 1797 and there is an extensive deer park.

The Orangery at Attingham is situated in the East Pavilion of the house and at the time of writing (1993) is awaiting restoration. It overlooks the river and the deer park.

Unfortunately there are no records to indicate the specific use of the Orangery or the fruits grown in it.

THE ORANGERY

Avington Park, Winchester, Hampshire, SO21 1DD

William Cobbett wrote of Avington that it was 'one of the prettiest places in the County' and indeed it is still true to-day. Charles II and George IV are amongst the former distinguished guests. It is an old red-brick house which was enlarged in 1670.

The Orangery was originally built of wood in the reign of Henry VIII and used as a banqueting hall, but burnt down in 1850. Crystal Palace was then the inspiration for it's new shape and it's re-construction using cast iron and glass. Two separate semi-circular glasshouses are joined by a covered walk-way which acts as a sheltered terrace.

There is a hypercourse underneath the floor, providing heat to enable the growing of unusual and out of season fruits. Unfortunately there are no records to indicate what varieties of fruit were actually grown. The Orangeries are no longer heated in winter but at the present time a giant fig tree climbs the wall of the right hand Orangery.

Attingham Park Orangery
National Trust Photographic Library

Avington Park Orangery

Belton House Orangery
National Trust Photographic Library / Neil Campbell-Sharp

Blickling Hall Orangery
National Trust Photographic Library

THE ORANGERY

Belton House, Near Grantham, Lincolnshire, NG32 2LS

Belton House was the crowning achievement of Restoration Country House Architecture and was built between 1684 and 1688 for Sir John Brownlow, heir to the fortunes of a successful Elizabethan Lawyer.

In 1810 the 1st Earl, Lord Brownlow's son, commissioned Jeffry Wyatville to redesign the area to the north-east of the house, which until then had been occupied by the kitchen garden. Wyatville's plans showed an elegant classical landscape with a large south facing Orangery which now stands near the site of the original house. Wyatville provided the designs for the south elevations and for the internal layout, showing the position of planting beds and the placement of two aviaries.

The Orangery is thought to have been completed about 1820 as records show that the small balusters on the roof were supplied by the Coade Manufactory at Lambeth in 1819-20. The first Earl, although chiefly remembered at Belton for his picture collection, was a pioneering gardener and developed a stove for warming tropical plants.

The interior of the Orangery survives intact, and is an example of the early use of cast-iron supporting structure, but the roof was replaced in 1857 with a totally glazed version, intended to capture more light at a time when the cultivation of tropical plants was becoming fashionable.

THE ORANGERY

Blickling Hall, Blickling, Norwich, NR11 6NF

Blickling Hall is a Great Jacobean red-bricked house. In 1767 the west front was built and a central inscription describes how Mary Anne Drury, Lord Buckinghamshire's first Countess, left her jewels to pay for it's completion. Unfortunately the work had been improperly bonded with the old work and the façade was rebuilt in the 1860's.

14

The Park, like the house is medieval in origin and there has been a major garden to the east of the house since Jacobean times, but each century has brought about substantial changes.

The Orangery was built in 1782, possibly by Samuel Wyatt. In 1781 Lord Buckinghamshire's agent Robert Copeman was opposed to the introduction of Wyatt and the building of the Orangery, preferring that "Mr Ivory be consulted as to the plan of the greenhouse rather than any newcomer." But the design of the Orangery strongly resembles Wyatt's Vine house at Holkham in it's reserved use of Coade stone plaques and it's marvellously delicate fanlights. Ivory's design for an Orangery with Gothic windows and a large blind upper story is dull by comparison.

Records show that in 1793 the Orangery contained exclusively orange trees and listed them as 15 large, 11 young and 6 dwarf oranges in a variety of boxes and tubs. 3 water pots, a water engine and a brazier, but to-day it remains un-heated and contains hardier plants.

THE ORANGERY

Burghley House, Stamford, Lincolnshire, PE9 3JY

Burghley House is the largest and grandest house of the Elizabethan age and has been the home of the Cecil family for over 400 years. It was built in 1587 by William Cecil, the first Lord Burghley and Lord High Treasurer to Queen Elizabeth I. The house is set in a deer park landscaped by 'Capability' Brown and is now the home of the Burghley Horse Trials.

'Capability' Brown also designed the beautiful Orangery in the Gothic Revival style for Lord Burghley, the 9th Earl of Exeter. This was built during the late 1760's, and constructed of Barnack Rag, a local limestone.

Unfortunately the history of the citrus collection is not known as there are no records in existence. To-day visitors can enjoy light refreshments in the charming surroundings of the Orangery overlooking the rose-beds and formal gardens.

Burghley House Orangery

Charlecote Park Orangery

Chatsworth Orangery
Chatsworth Settlement Trustees

17

THE ORANGERY

Charlecote Park, Wellesbourne, Warwick, CV35 9ER

There has been a home for the Lucy family at Charlecote Park since 1247, with the present house built by the Lucy family in 1550. Visitors to the house included Elizabeth I. Refurbishment in the Elizabethan Revival style of the house at Charlecote Park took place in 1830.

The park was landscaped by 'Capability' Brown and supports a herd of red and fallow deer, reputedly poached by Shakespeare, and a flock of Jacob sheep, first introduced in 1756.

The Orangery at Charlecote Park was not built until 1857 when the house belonged to Henry Spencer Lucy. It is known to have housed the exotic plants that had been raised in the hot houses enclosed in the walled garden. Today refreshments are served in the Orangery.

THE ORANGERY

Chatsworth House, Bakewell, Derbyshire, DE4 1PP

The 6th Duke of Devonshire's plan for the north wing of Chatsworth House was for it to end with the Sculpture Gallery, but when he 'got bit by gardening' due to the enthusiasm engendered by his head gardener and friend Joseph Paxton (1803-65), the Orangery was added.

The records show it was visited by the Prince and Princess of Wales in 1872 and a picture of the occasion shows how beautifully it was illuminated.

Sculpture and tender plants shared it happily for years. Now it contains a shop, but there is still room for a copy of the Medici Vase by Lorenzo Bartolini (1777-1850). The Medici Vase is a giant quartz crystal discovered during excavations for the tunnel through the Simpson Pass.

The Orangery also houses the State Coach which was brought to Chatsworth in the 1890's by Louise Duchess, wife of the 8th Duke and was used by the present Duke and Duchess and their son Lord Hartington, then aged nine, at the coronation of Queen Elizabeth II in

1953. Lord Hartington was page to his grandmother, Mary Duchess of Devonshire, who was Mistress of the Robes to Her Majesty.

Although citrus fruits are still grown at Chatsworth they are housed in a modern greenhouse built by the present Duke and the Orangery itself is used as the visitor's shop. Citrus trees were housed in the Orangery up until the First World War.

THE ORANGERY

Dyrham Park, Nr Chippenham, Bristol, Avon, SN14 8ER

This late 17th century house is built, like many others in a splendid deer park. It houses the Blathwayt furniture collection and Dutch paintings in a fine series of panelled rooms.

The Dyrham Orangery was unusual in that it was built directly on to and connecting with the house itself. In this position, as Repton pointed out, it effectively hides the stable block and offices.

The Orangery was almost certainly designed by Talman, and was probably started in 1701, together with the corresponding arcading on the north side of the house, 'vanishing into the side of the hill, in a curious collision between symmetry and geography' as *Country Life's* author wrote.

This is one of the earliest examples in England of the monumentally treated Orangery. The round-headed windows and the massive coupled Tuscan columns were doubtless copied from the Orangery at Versailles, but the quoins around the windows and the heavy frost-work keystones have more of the character of Italian mannerism.

The roof behind is hidden by a panelled parapet and a balustrade. The proportions of this superstructure are a little clumsy. The exhortation carved on the convex frieze, *servare modum, finemque tueri, naturamque sequi*, is an adaptation of a line from Lucan's Pharsalia. It may be translated as: 'observe moderation, keep the end in view, follow the law of nature'.

19

Dyrham Park Orangery
National Trust Photographic Library / Angelo Hornak

Dunham Massey Orangery.
National Trust Photographic Library / Geoff Morgan

20

Ham House Orangery
National Trust Photographic Library

21

THE ORANGERY

Dunham Massey, Altringham, Cheshire, WA14 4SJ

Dunham Massey is a fine 18th Century house with Georgian and Edwardian interiors. The extensive gardens have recently been restored. There is a wooded deer park, with a herd of fallow deer and a working Elizabethan water mill which is powered from the moat.

The Orangery at Dunham Massey is set on the edge of the lawn in what is now a largely Victorian pleasure ground. It was constructed of brick and built about 1780 although the architect is unknown.

The interior of the Orangery has a stone floor and the walls are covered with a number of climbers including the arbutilons 'Ashford Red' and 'Canary Bird' and on the exterior, roses of the 19th century Noisette type.

The Orangery was repaired in 1983 and myrtles have now been placed in free-standing tubs, following a design found at Dunham.

These are placed outside in summer.

THE ORANGERY

Ham House, Richmond, Surrey, TW10 7RS

Ham House is an outstanding Stuart house built about 1610 but was enlarged and enriched in the most up-to-date style of the time by the Duke and Duchess of Lauderdale in the 1670's.

The Orangery at Ham House is considered to be the oldest surviving Orangery in the country. Reference was made to it by John Evelyn who recalled seeing "Orangeries" at Ham House as early as 1678. Part of the Orangery was converted into living accommodation in the 1950's and the building was partially turned into a tea room and kitchen in about 1975.

Ham House, at the time of writing (1993) is currently undergoing building work and it is hoped that it may be possible to restore the Orangery in due course to it's original use. The gardens have recently been restored to their 17th century plan.

22

THE ORANGERY

Hanbury Hall, Nr Droitwich, Hereford & Worcester, WR9 7EA

This William and Mary style house built of red brick and completed in 1701 for a wealthy lawyer, has outstanding painted ceilings and staircase by Sir James Thornhill.

The Orangery at Hanbury Hall is one of the few that is still used to house a citrus collection. There are eight trees, four Washington Navel orange and four lemons. These are grown in Versailles tubs, with the orange trees placed outside in the summer, and the lemon trees kept in the Orangery all year round. The orange trees have been at Hanbury Hall for many years, but the lemon trees are a new introduction.

The citrus trees were normally just overwintered in the Orangery and were kept warm with a heated back wall system, but later a Victorian system was introduced providing piped hot water around the inside of the Orangery.

It is thought the Orangery was built about 1730 during the time of Bowater Vernon (1683-1735). It is very similar in external appearance to many others, having the tall sash windows, characteristic of the period. It is brick built and measures about 66 ft 6 ins by 20 ft wide. It is in a similar style to the Hall and is a very attractive building adorned with stone carvings of fruit basket, flowers and wreaths in the pediment and has urn and pineapple finials.

Among Bowater Vernon's papers which are kept at Worcester Records Office, is a 'Method of raising orange trees from Genoa' It would not be unreasonable to assume therefore, that the original collection of citrus trees must have came from Genoa.

Hanbury Hall Orangery
National Trust Photographic Library / David Hunter

The Orangery at the Royal Botanic Gardens Kew

THE ORANGERY

Royal Botanic Gardens, Kew, Richmond, Surrey, TW9 3AB

In 1761, Augusta, Dowager Princess of Wales had Sir William Chambers build the Orangery at Kew to improve the provision for a collection of citrus that had belonged to her late husband Frederick up until his death in 1751. He had been growing orange trees at the instigation of the Earl of Bute.

The Orangery is the largest classical building in the Gardens and is made of brick, but covered with stucco to look like stone. The front is 145 feet in length and the walls are 31 inches thick. The interior is 142 feet long, 30 feet wide and 25 feet high. At the back there were originally two furnaces to heat flues laid under the pavement. The end walls were originally solid, the glass doors being added in 1842. The plaster ceiling was replaced in the 1950's by emulsion-painted plaster board.

The Orangery's charm derives from it's well-balanced proportions and the line pattern formed by the channels of stucco and the bars of the windows. It was however, badly designed for growing oranges because of the insufficiency of light from the windows and the incompatibility between the building's structure and the warm atmosphere needed for fruiting. Orange trees were grown in tubs and were housed during the winter in the Orangery and were put outside in summer. *The Horticultural Journal* for October 1837 said, "the Orangery is at present almost completely filled with rare plants of the Araucaria and other genera...[and] almost innumerable rows of orange trees."

In 1841, when Kew Gardens was taken over by the nation, the orange trees were moved to Kensington Palace. In 1863 the Orangery became a museum for timbers from different parts of the Empire for the Great Exhibition of 1862. In 1959 Sir George Taylor the Director of the Royal Botanic Gardens at that time, had it restored for the bi-centenary commemoration of Princess Augusta's original botanic garden.

The necessary humidity for keeping orange trees which were still being housed in the Orangery along with other plants, caused dry-rot, so the Orangery was again restored by Professor John Heslop-Harrison, Director from 1971, for £14,500 and re-opened on 5th May 1972 as a public exhibition centre for the Gardens' scientific work and to display prints, paintings and drawings from the Kew collection.

THE ORANGERY

Montacute House, Montacute, Somerset, TA15 6XP

The Orangery is situated in the south west corner of the north garden with an orientation of north-south. Light is obtained through the glazed timber roof and the east front. The rest is wall, built out of honey coloured ham stone. Ventilation is by means of the double doors at the centre of the east front and one south window each side of the door.

The interior floor dimensions are approximately 13.25 metres x 6 metres and the height to the eaves is 4.3 metres and to the ridge 5.7 metres.

There is some confusion as to the age of this Orangery. In 1778 the then owner, Edward Phelips recorded putting out the orange trees. A plan of 1825 shows a small building on or close to the site. However a sketch plan by the head gardener Mr Pridham dated c1848 includes the Orangery which is described as the 'New Greenhouse'. Whatever the date, the style is of the 18th century.

To-day the interior is beautifully laid out. There is a perimeter path of hamstone flags which are laid to create narrow beds at the base of the walls on three sides. There is also a central path and on either side of this a raised bed which is rectangular, but for an inward curve to the north west corner of the south bed, and the south west corner of the north bed. In these beds are grown large standard fuchsias 'Lena' (6 in each) under which are currrently white petunias and the whole is surrounded by a clipped ivy hedge.

The narrow beds at the base of the walls are planted with *Jasminum Polyanthum, Fatshedera, Schizophagma and Lonicera Sempervirens.* All are trained on the walls and beneath these grow ferns.

One important feature is a large mound of hamstone built centrally on the wall terminating the central path. On this grows maiden hair fern kept moist by a fountain spout at the top which drips water down into a pool at the base. At one time, water would have dripped out of the pool basin onto central heating pipes beneath a grille in the Orangery floor, thus increasing the humidity. The Orangery is no longer heated other than for frost protection which is provided by thermostatically controlled fan heaters in winter.

Montacute House Orangery
National Trust Photographic Library / Neil Campbell-Sharp

Longleat House Orangery
Reproduced by kind permission of The Marquess of Bath

Saltram House Orangery
National Trust Photographic Library / Nick Meers

THE ORANGERY

Longleat, Warminster, Wiltshire, BA12 7NW

The house at Longleat was built in 1580 by Sir John Thynne on the site of a former priory. It was the first truly magnificent Elizabethan House to be built in the Renaissance style and the Thynne family still reside there to-day. Running through the estate was a millstream or watercourse converted to a chain of lakes by Lancelot 'Capability' Brown who remodeled the park in 1757 and swept away the formal gardens. The millstream was called the long 'leat'.

The Orangery at Longleat lies in the north garden just behind the house. Designed by Sir Jeffry Wyatville, it has nine large windows and dates from the early 19th century. In front of the Orangery are the remaining formal gardens. Orange trees are still grown in the Orangery at Longleat, but it has also been used in the recent past to grow orchids.

Wyatville also contributed to the extensive alterations to Longleat House itself, a new stable block, boat-house, cottage orné and an entrance lodge of the same period.

Longleat was the first stately home to be opened to the public in 1949 and in 1966 became the first Safari Park and wild animal reserve outside Africa.

THE ORANGERY

Saltram House, Plympton, Plymouth, Devon, PL7 3UH

This is a George II house built around and incorporating the remnants of a late Tudor Mansion, set in a landscaped park. It has two exceptional rooms by Robert Adam, a Great Kitchen and beautiful gardens.

Henry Stockman designed the Orangery at Saltram House, which was built between 1773 and 1775. Originally constructed of timber, with a tiled roof, it has seven very large sash windows to let in the light. A fire in 1932 caused severe damage, but it was restored between 1956 and 1961.

The orange trees were originally purchased from Genoa, Italy. They were displayed outside in the Grove during the summer from 29th May, which is known as 'Oak Apple Day', until the second Wednesday in October. This was traditionally the day the Tavistock Goose Fair was held.

When the trees were outside, the Orangery itself was used as a place of quiet contemplation for the family of the day and as a place to entertain estate workers and tenants. Niches and statues decorated the Orangery to make it an attractive place in the summer.

THE ORANGERY

Tatton Park, Knutsford, Cheshire, WA16 6QN

Set in 1,000 acres of deer park, this 19th century fine Georgian Mansion was built by Samuel and Lewis Wyatt and is the seat of the late Lord Egerton of Tatton. The house is beautifully decorated and furnished, and houses many family collections.

The 50 acres of gardens at Tatton Park include an authentic Japanese garden, fernery, rose garden, arboretum, rhododendrons and azaleas, with an Italian garden and an Orangery.

The Orangery is of an unusual design, but magnificent in it's appearance. It has very large windows all around the building instead of the plain back wall. The early planting history of the Orangery is unclear and at present (1993) it is undergoing restoration after which it will again house orange trees.

Tatton Park Orangery
National Trust Photographic Library / Mark Fiennes

Lyme Park Orangery
National Trust Photographic Library

THE ORANGERY

Lyme Park, Disley, Stockport, Cheshire, SK12 2NX

Lyme Park has been the home of the Legh family for 600 years. Part of the Elizabethan house has survived but alterations were carried out in the 1730's by Giacomo Leoni and later by Lewis Wyatt. This has given the Hall a blend of Elizabethan, Georgian and Regency architecture.

The extensive 1377 acres of designated parkland is home to a herd of both red and fallow deer. There are breathtaking views of the Peak District and the Cheshire Plain.

The 17 acres of terraced and formal gardens at Lyme Park house the Orangery which was designed by Lewis Wyatt and completed in 1862 by Alfred Derbyshire. It was built of sandstone with a large central bay flanked on each side with huge windows. The roof originally had a large central dome under which grew a palm tree. The palm tree eventually outgrew the height and literally pushed the roof off. Both the palm tree and the roof dome were removed and a new glass roof was installed.

The Orangery is cunningly designed. The photograph views the Orangery from the pleasure grounds, but it backs onto the working area of the house which includes a courtyard and brew-house where ale was brewed and from which the excess heat was used to warm the Orangery. There is a series of underground passages in this area where servants of the house could move about unseen. One of these links the Orangery with the kitchen.

In the 1950's the Orangery was used as a cafeteria, but has since been restored and replanted. It houses a fig tree and two 200 year old camelias inter-twined to look like one, the identity of which has confounded the experts. Formal bedding has been laid out and a tiered water fountain has been installed. This provides some humidity in the summer but the actual sound of the water has proved an added attraction.

THE ORANGERY

Ickworth, The Rotunda, Horringer, Bury St Edmunds, Suffolk, IP29 5QE

The House at Ickworth took many years to complete. It was begun in 1794 and finished in 1830. The style of the house is most unusual, being an eccentric elliptical rotunda connected by two curved corridors to flanking wings.

The Orangery was originally intended in 1829 as a vast picture gallery attached to the house, forming part of a wing, but it was not finished at the time of building.

There are nine bays and the floor length windows lead out on to the terrace. There are formal gardens, herbaceous borders and an extensive deer park.

To-day the Orangery is used to house fuchsias and scented geraniums but there are no records to indicate if at any time it housed citrus fruits.

THE ORANGERY

Burton Constable Hall, Near Hull, Humberside, HU11 4LN

Burton Constable Hall is a magnificent Elizabethan House, built around 1570 and is the home of the Lord Paramount of Holderness. Like many stately homes, it houses an outstanding collection of paintings and furniture, but also has a unique collection of scientific instruments collected in the eighteenth-century by William Constable. The parklands were designed by 'Capability' Brown.

The Orangery was designed by Thomas Atkinson of York and the original architectural drawings are held in the collection at the Hall. It was built during 1788-89 and measures 61 feet long. The artificial stone ornaments on the top were supplied by Messrs Coade & Co in 1789.

Ickworth House Orangery
National Trust Photographic Library / Mark Fiennes

Burton Constable Hall Orangery
The Burton Constable Foundation

Kensington Palace Orangery

37

The Orangery to-day still houses a few orange and lemon trees but is generally used as a hot-house for geraniums and other plants. In the 1970's the Orangery served as an aviary for exotic birds.

With it's glass frontage. the orangery is completely accessible for viewing from the outside, but is not actually open to the public at present.

THE ORANGERY

Kensington Palace, Kensington, London

Originally called Nottingham House and built as a Jacobean Mansion in about 1605, it was purchased by William III and Mary in 1689. The house was extensively altered by Sir Christopher Wren and renamed.

The Orangery was built in 1704 for Queen Anne and was designed by Hawksmoor and Vanbrugh. It has the finest architectural interior at Kensington. Built of red brick, the entrance and the door opposite are flanked by fluted Corinthian columns. A finely carved cornice adorns the high walls which are white painted wood panels. These reflect the light from the south facing large windows.

At each end of the Orangery are circular rooms in which are now displayed a pair of large vases sculptured in the late seventeenth-century for the gardens at Hampton Court. The many niches are filled with statues and eighteenth-century copies of Roman busts.

The Orangery is today used as an elegant tea room. The white walls contrast well with the green foliage of the Orange trees. Most of the trees are placed outside for the summer and stand on the original terrace of Portland stone.

The Orangery overlooks an avenue of bay trees, holly bushes and formal gardens.

THE ORANGERY

Merley Bird Gardens, Wimborne, Dorset.

The walls which to-day enclose the Merley Bird Gardens were one part of the setting for a truly English piece of history. The story starts towards the end of the Civil War when an ardent Royalist named Ralph Willett saw that his cause was lost and left for the West Indies, where he made a fortune in the sugar trade.

Years later his grandson returned to England and bought the Merley Estate in 1751. He built the present house which took 8 years to complete and the young Ralph Willett, along with John Nash, oversaw the design and construction of a spacious walled garden at the same time. On the south side of the garden he built the Orangery whose façade remains a fine example of artistic bricklaying.

The estate of Merley was auctioned, sold and divided many times over the years and the walled garden was sold in 1967. The new owners constructed many aviaries, ponds and enclosures and opened Merley Bird Gardens to the public for the first time in June 1968.

Orange trees were still over wintered in the Orangery up until the 1920's, but after extensive refurbishment it is now used as a tea-room.

The tower which is adjacent to the Orangery was built as a water tower to store water which had been pumped up from the lake. This was then used to water the walled garden.

There were three bays to the Orangery with the typical large arched windows, but these have now been replaced. The only photograph that is available shows the back wall of the Orangery with one large door.

Two statues that were housed in the alcoves shown at each side of the door, had been sold but were later found and bought back. They now stand in another part of the garden. Their inspiration or representation are not known, but they are affectionately known as the 'uglies'.

Merley Bird Garden Orangery

The 'Uglies' at Merley Bird Garden

Margam Park Orangery in Winter West Glamorgan County Council

THE ORANGERY

Margam Park, Port Talbot, West Glamorgan, South Wales.

The Great Orangery at Margam Park, is a rare beauty thanks to the extensive restoration work carried out by West Glamorgan County Council in 1977. The Orangery stands at 327 feet long and is the largest in the UK.

It was originally built between 1786 and 1790 by Thomas Mansel Talbot to house a large citrus collection which included oranges, lemons and citrons. The origin of these trees is steeped in legend, there being several versions of how the trees came to Margam. More than one version says they were on route from Spain, but the ship was wrecked off the coast of Glamorgan, and the trees were rescued or claimed, along with the other cargo, by the family of the day, the Mansels.

The earliest records at Margam which mention the existence of the trees, dates back to 1711, and comprise a note in the accounts of the day, that 'the citrus trees have been put out'. They were traditionally put outside in May for the summer and then brought in during October for the winter.

The records show that the trees were both numerous and large, comprising:

2   large Sittrons (citrons) about 12 feet in diameter
2   small Sittrons
1   large Bergamot, about 10 feet in diameter
11   small Bergamots
3   large Lemons, about 10 feet in diameter
1   large Lime, about 7 feet in diameter
6   small Lemons, some 6, some 5, some 3 feet in diameter
10   large Chaney (China) Oranges, some 8, 10, 12 feet in diameter
5   small China Oranges
13   large Sivel (Seville) Oranges, some 7, some 10 feet in diameter, some 13 feet high
6   small Sivel Oranges, about 4 feet in diameter
11   Lemon stocks, to be budded. In pots.

In 1750, the last of the Mansel family died without a male heir and the property passed to The Reverend Thomas Talbot, who when he died, made mention of the citrus collection in his will, bequeathing them to his son Thomas Mansel Talbot who was a renowned traveller. Rome became the inspiration for his Orangery which is a masterpiece of eighteenth-century architecture, magnificently ornamental in appearance and superbly functional in design. The depth of the Orangery is only 30 feet. The 27 tall round headed windows made the most of the winter light which could then reach the whole interior of the building, giving maximum benefit to the citrus trees.

The construction is of carved stone with the five central windows standing proud of the main building and the carved garlands and classical bukrania above, breaking the long line of the roof. The back wall housed the fireplaces and the heat was circulated by means of underfloor flues. A large arched doorway set in the back wall allowed for easy moving of even the tallest trees.

At each end of the Orangery is a pedimented pavilion where Thomas Mansel Talbot displayed his Roman antiquities collected on his travels. The west pavilion, called the library pavilion had a marble fireplace and elaborate plasterwork decorating the walls. In here were displayed carved alabaster vases and models of Roman buildings. While in the west pavilion, which was less elaborately decorated, were the displays of statuary.

The stone for the Orangery was taken from Thomas Mansel Talbot's own quarry at Pyle, and the building took more than four years to complete. The architect was Anthony Keck who had created Talbot's villa at Penrice. Most of the materials and tools used were from local sources, but some were brought from Bristol and Gloucester. Most of the labourers and skilled craftsmen were local.

A collection of citrus trees were preserved at Margam up until the outbreak of the second world war, but then the Orangery was requisitioned for military use and the trees were placed outside. They did not survive the winter weather and died. A new collection of citrus trees was introduced after the war and were housed in the Orangery until ownership of Margam passed into the hands of West Glamorgan County Council.

The trees are now housed in the Citrus House, formally known as the 'Orange Wall'. The collection of citrus trees has been enlarged and a spray of Orange Blossom from the Margam trees was placed in the carriage in which Their Royal Highnesses the Prince and Princess of Wales drove from St Paul's after their wedding.

Margam Park Orangery in Summer West Glamorgan County Council

Mount Edgcumbe Orangery City of Plymouth & Cornwall County Council

THE ORANGERY

Mount Edgcumbe Country Park,
Cremyll, Torpoint, Cornwall, PL10 1HZ

Stretching along 10 miles of spectacular coastline from Plymouth to Whitsand bay, the park contains one of only three Grade I Historic Gardens in Cornwall. It was designed 240 years ago and includes a deer park and formal gardens. The house has been the home of the Edgcumbe family for 400 years and having been devastated in 1941, has recently been refurbished and redecorated to reflect the late 18th century.

The Orangery is perhaps appropriately situated in the Italian Garden and was designed by Thomas Pitt 2nd Lord Camelford (1737-1793). It's original size was 100 ft long by 30 ft wide.

The first trees in it's collection were supposed to have been brought back to this country by Richard, 2nd Lord Edgcumbe (1716-1761), from Constantinople in 1744, where he had gone to escape his creditors. In 1760, it was recorded that there were 25 trees in the collection but by 1809, nearly 50 years later, the collection of citrus trees was considered to be among the finest in England. They were very numerous, and in summer ranged along the sides of the walks, forming avenues in every direction.

By 1882 the Gardeners Chronicle mentioned "....The plants are in magnificent health and are well furnished with fruits, indeed the whole collection, irrespective of variety is remarkable for the quantities of fruit borne upon each plant. If any exception can be made, it must be awarded to the beautiful bushes of the Myrtle-leaved Orange, which are particularly ornamental, many of the taller growing kinds are close upon 20ft high...."

This notable Orangery was illustrated on many occasions in the 19th century by Nicholas Condy, some of whose watercolours are in the Royal Collection at Windsor Castle.

Towards the end of the 19th century the orange trees outgrew the building and it was considerably enlarged. It suffered extensive damage during the second world war and was refurbished by Adrian Gilbert Scott.

The original orange trees died during the war, but in 1990 new ones were purchased and these trees are placed in the Italian Garden each summer. The Orangery itself is now used as a restaurant for the Park.

THE ORANGERY

Woburn Abbey, Woburn, Bedfordshire, MK43 0TP

Woburn Abbey is over 800 years old, built by a Cistercian monk. Hugh de Bolbec who founded the monastery in 1145. It was inhabited by monks until 1538, when it was confiscated by Henry VIII and given to the 1st Earl. However it was the 4th Earl who made it the family home during the 1620's. The Dukedom was created in 1694 and Woburn Abbey became the home of The Dukes of Bedford and has remained so for nearly 400 years.

The Orangery was built between 1789 and 1790 by Henry Holland for the 5th Duke and was linked to the Abbey by a covered passage. In 1802 Holland added the Temple of Liberty as a setting for the busts of leading political figures of the day and in 1818 the Orangery was enlarged by Jeffry Wyatville to house the 6th Duke's collection of marble statuary and reliefs.

The centre of the Orangery is supported by eight marble columns topped with corinthian capitals, dating from the 2nd century AD. These were found in Rome at the beginning of the 19th century during excavations of the site reputed to be Hadrian's villa.

Around 1800 pieces of sculpture appeared amongst the plants and it was then converted into what was, at the time, a very fashionable Sculpture Gallery.

By 1820 all the plants must have been removed as the floor was then paved with Purbeck Stone and inlaid with Devonshire Marble. No record is available of the citrus trees that were grown in the Orangery at that time.

In 1968 the Orangery was restored and is now used as a magnificent setting for a vast range of functions, including Exhibitions, Concerts and Receptions.

Woburn Abbey Orangery

Powis Castle Orangery National Trust Photographic Library

THE ORANGERY

Powis Castle, Welshpool, Powys, Wales, SY21 8RF

Powis Castle was the Medieval stronghold of the Welsh Princes of Upper Powys and was built c1200. It has been the home of the Herbert family since 1587. In 1784 Lord Powis's daughter, Lady Henrietta Herbert, married Edward Clive, the eldest son of Clive of India. The Clive fortune paid for long overdue repairs to Powis. The garden and park were also improved. This marriage also brought to Powis part of Clive of India's fine collection of old master pictures, French and English furniture and Indian curiosities.

The extensive parallel terraces hanging over each other, are of such rarity that Powis Castle is one of the very few places in Britain where the grandeur of a seventeenth-century baroque garden can be fully appreciated.

The concept of the terraces derives from sixteenth-century Italy and was introduced to Northern Europe by the French. The actual design of the terraces is attributed to William Winde who is known to have constructed similar garden terraces at Cliveden, and who is credited with the late seventeenth-century alterations to the castle.

The Orangery is set into the terrace and forms part of it. Built of red brick it has a central columned entrance with three large windows at each side. The balustrade and Liliputian statues form the wall of the terrace walk above and were much admired by Sir John Cullum in 1774 along with the 'clipt yews' which have since grown into fantastic shapes, never envisaged when they were planted.

In 1732 John Loveday had noted an "abundance of fruit" and a "good brick Greenhouse, in it a very large Aloe, one of it's leaves 4 foot long". This is thought to refer to the Orangery, which is no longer heated, but which has the remains of the furnace alongside.

Orange trees were often referred to as the 'wall trees' and this was mentioned in 1771 when Lady Powis requested: "That Mr Jones the Gardener prepare the ground on the several Terras's for the Wall Trees immediately, and Cut down and plant such Trees as he has reported to Lady Powis proper for these walls."

THE ORANGERIES

Hampton Court Palace, London

Thomas Wolsey was the first minister to King Henry VIII. In 1514 Wolsey had Hampton Court built at great cost and filled it with priceless treasures. King Henry VIII coveted Hampton Court and in 1525 Wolsey thought it prudent to bestow it to Henry VIII as a gift. However Wolsey lost favour four years later with the King and was sentenced to death. He died on the way to his execution.

Magnificent as it was, Henry VIII made extensive alterations to the Palace. He built a Great Hall, which survives intact to-day, a library, state apartments and also made provision for sporting pastimes which included tennis.

The Palace was again dramatically altered during the joint reign of William and Mary. who commissioned Christopher Wren to redesign the Palace. He had two courts pulled down and a third remodelled to produce a grand classical renaissance style mansion in Portland stone and red-brick. Two separate courts were built, one for each monarch.

The gardens were re-designed in the Formal French style and an Orangery was built in each court. King William already grew citrus fruits in his gardens in Het Loo, Holland and had trees brought over from there.

King William's Orangery is set immediately under the Kings apartments and would have originally had a black and white tiled floor. This has since been replaced with Swedish limestone purple and grey tiles. The many and large windows allow for the low winter sun to reflect to the back of the Orangery, bringing maximum benefit to the trees. There are no windows in the rear wall, only a door and the orangery itself was heated with two stoves. Orangeries of the day were often referred to as 'Greenhouses' because of the green plants that they contained.

There is still a collection of citrus trees grown at Hampton Court and housed in this Orangery during the winter. In summer, the trees are placed outside on the terrace. The formal gardens in front of the King's apartments are at the present time, being restored. There is much excavation going on to determine the original layout.

The Orangery at Hampton Court
under the King's Apartments

The Lower Orangery at Hampton Court
built near the Queen's Apartments

Felbrigg Hall Orangery
National Trust Photographic Library / Marianne Majerus

The Orangery built for Queen Mary stands in front of the Queen's Apartments and was built to replace the three hot houses that stood in the former pond yard. It is often referred to as the 'Lower Orangery'. At the time of writing (1993) this Orangery is being used to house a collection of paintings that have been recently restored and the atmospheric conditions are carefully controlled.

Near-by is the greenhouse that houses the 'Great Vine'. This vine was planted by 'Capability' Brown in 1768 and still produces grapes today.

THE ORANGERY

Felbrigg Hall, Roughton, Norwich NR11 8PR

Felbrigg Hall is one of the finest seventeenth-century houses in Norfolk and it still has it's original eighteenth-century furniture and pictures. It has an outstanding library, walled garden and restored dovecot.

The Orangery was built on the north side of the parterre, with seven tall south facing windows. It was built by Ashe Windham but although the drawings are still in the archives, no signature is attached for identification of the architect. The design though is in exact harmony with existing designs and in the same beautiful precise brickwork.

The records show that Ashe's mother, Katherine seemed to have contributed largely to the building of the Orangery, writing to him in February 1705 as follows "I design to find sashes, workmanship, shutters, doors, pavements for the orange house, you find bricke, lime, timber, tile and carriage" and she recorded in her account book in 1707 "My son laid out on my account for ye Orange house £261.16s.11d."

In 1958 the roof which had fallen into great disrepair was reconstructed on the basis of the original drawings and the cornice which had entirely disappeared, was replaced. The parterre in front of the Orangery must have been swept away early in the vogue for 'natural landscape'. Lady Beauchamps Proctor who visited Felbrigg in 1764 found "not much garden, but a very good greenhouse out of which the gardener gave each of us a fine nosegay of orange-flowers, geraniums etc. which travelled with us the rest of our tour."

The Orangery, though unheated, houses a collection of camellias, some of considerable size and age. These are under-planted with a variety of interesting hardy ferns, and in front, with the scented rhododendron *'Fragrantissimum'*

There is an area around the Orangery that is known as the 'American Garden'. This term originated from the early and very special collection of truly American plants, introduced from the new world in the eighteenth-century.

THE MODERN CONSERVATORY

Very few of us can these days readily afford a purpose built Orangery to house our citrus collections, but this does not mean we cannot grow Oranges and Lemons if we choose to do so. Citrus trees require frost free conditions in winter as they are still actively growing, and citrus fruits are winter ripening so you should be eating your fruit from October to March. The ideal compromise would be a modern conservatory.

Many people have in recent years built a conservatory attached to their house. Some consider it to be an extension of the lounge, some as the added dining room they have always required, and some use it as an indoor extension to their garden. The use to which a conservatory can be put is endless.

If you are now considering building a conservatory, you will be met with a minefield of conflicting advice. It will be as well to try and resolve some of the questions you have before you start, in order to determine exactly what your requirements are.

The modern conservatory is available in a variety of materials, typically; Softwood, Hardwood, Aluminium and PVC-u. Your choice of materials may be pre-determined by the style of house to which it will be attached but we will consider each on it's merits so that you will be fully aware of the choices available to you.

Softwood
Although a popular choice for many nineteenth-century glass houses, currently softwood conservatories are often the cheapest option for 'custom' made designs. However most softwood used today is of the 'forced grown' variety and it is not unusual for external timber-work such as windows and fascias to need replacement after as little as four years.

A timber construction will require maintenance and decorating. Modern micro-porous stains and paints have reduced the effort required but you should allow for redecoration every two to three years to give maximum protection from the weather.

If you decide to grow plants in your conservatory that require fixing to the structure, such as climbing plants, this will make the maintenance much more difficult. The high humidity required by some plants grown

Internal View of a Modern Conservatory Trafalgar Home Improvements Ltd/Graeme Grant-Willis

in conservatories will cause the wood to split and twist. A softwood conservatory then has little to recommend it in the long run.

Hardwood.

Choosing a hardwood conservatory is favoured by many for it's natural feel and appearance. It seems to suit certain building designs. However for those who are environmentally conscious, using timbers from the rain forests can pose other problems. It would be wise to check the source of the material as there are now 'managed' hardwood forests in Africa which have been developed as a renewable source of timber for the building trade. European and North American timber is also available.

Maintenance for hardwood will be the same as for softwood. It is essential that the maintenance schedule be adhered to, because if the hardwood is allowed to deteriorate and develop 'blackening' the amount of work required to return it to it's original finish will be intensive and time consuming.

As with softwood, particular attention must be paid to maintaining the glazing rebates and beads. If these are allowed to deteriorate and water seepage occurs, premature failure of double glazing units will result.

Hardwood conservatories will provide a longer life than softwood equivalents, however the maintenance is still a discouraging factor for those who prefer to spend their spare time in relaxation and hobbies, as opposed to hard work and maintenance.

Aluminium

Aluminium conservatories offer traditional styling elements such as dentil mouldings and cresting within a low maintenance material, but in some locations however, the high gloss finish provided by powder coating can look entirely inappropriate and too modern.

An environmental consideration to this material is that vast open cast mines in Australia, Brazil and Canada add nothing to conservation nor does the high energy requirement for processing bauxite into aluminium billet and fabricated sections.

It is important to realise that there are two distinct categories of Aluminium conservatories. The cheapest types are still fabricated from solid or non-insulated sections. These tend to be found at garden centres and are most commonly used as 'lean-to' designs at the lower end of the price range. They are usually single glazed and do not allow for re-positioning of doors and windows to suit your specific requirement.

This type has it's origins in greenhouse design and should best be viewed as a greenhouse rather than an extension of the home. The wild variations of temperature experienced in single glazed conservatories makes environment control prohibitively expensive and condensation on aluminium of this nature is a constant problem.

The finish should be anodised or powder coated colour that should not require repainting in normal use. It is worth noting though that should a powder coating be chipped it is essential to retouch the effected area immediately. Your supplier should have the appropriate material to do this.

Another point to remember is that salt spray can have a disastrous effect on the aluminium and some manufacturers do not offer any form of guarantee if an aluminium conservatory is erected within 400 metres of the coast. Others will give only limited warranties if the framework may be subject to salt spray. It is important that any salt spray is washed off at the first opportunity to prevent permanent damage.

The second type of aluminium conservatory was introduced to compete with Hardwood and PVC-u, specifically to provide a room for household use. The frame sections are clad with PVC-u to provide thermal insulation of the aluminium in an effort to reduce the incidence of frame condensation.

A properly developed aluminium conservatory will not require the use of a hardwood sub-frame and any design requiring one would be best avoided at all costs, as it is likely that what is on offer is little more than aluminium window sections not specifically designed for the purpose. In the storms of 1987 and 1990 which lashed the South of England, the haphazard design of these particular conservatories were shown to be unsound and even dangerous.

PVC-u.
This is now the single most popular material for the modern conservatory. The frame material has the highest natural insulation properties of any man made section in the conservatory field. Environmental and condensation control is therefore easier and much more economically achieved. If it is your intention to use the conservatory for plants requiring high humidity, PCV-u will not be adversely affected.

59

Like aluminium, the frames will accommodate much wider sealed double glazing and provide optimum insulation. Until recently, however, the drawback with PVC-u was it's rather hard appearance and the limitation of only being available in a white finish. There is no justifiable reason today for this still to be the case. Decorative crests and finials externally and traditional style finishing trims internally, now combine to give a far softer appearance to this material.

Colour finishes in matt or gloss are available as are various shades of wood-grain effect. These are now proven to be totally reliable. It is a very useful guide that when talking to potential suppliers, if you meet resistance to any suggestion of using wood-grain or colour, even if this is indicated as being available only with a lesser guarantee than the white finish, shop elsewhere. If their frame system has been properly tested and proven, there would be no expectation for you to accept a dearer product, for less commitment from them. As with aluminium, however, there is a distinct variation in the quality of product available.

No PVC-u conservatory should be considered if any part of the vertical elevations are externally glazed. Simply put, the glass in the doors and windows should not be secured by an external glazing bead. Despite the best endeavours of the frame suppliers no answer has been found to provide a design that will resist a reasonably proficient thief. One solution offered was to use what amounts to double sided sticking tape to hold the glass in situ if the head is removed. The obvious problem with this however, is how do you replace the glass at anything like a reasonable cost if the pane were accidentally broken?

Another common compromise in PVC-u is related to the fitment of French doors. Many systems do not have the appropriate parts to make an outward opening type without resorting to using an inward opening set and then installing them 'back to front'. Likewise with both types, it is not unusual to find that the threshold of the door stands proud of the floor by up to 4 inches. In either case do not accept the compromise. There are sufficient good designs available for you not to put up with this inconvenience.

On initial inspection PVC-u appears to be the least environmentally acceptable material, however when all issues have been considered, many authorities have reviewed and reversed their initially hostile attitude to this material. PVC-u requires no maintenance other than occasional washing over with soapy water. For the typical household, PVC-u has much to recommend it.

A Modern Conservatory can be designed to suit any house or roof height. Trafalgar Home Improvements Ltd/Graeme Grant-Willis.

If you wish to secure hanging plants or creepers from the frame these will not have to be disturbed for any maintenance, nor will you have to rehouse your plants to prevent damage by the fumes of a re-varnish or painting.

Having considered the appropriate material for your conservatory structure and decided the use to which you will put your conservatory, there are a few other points to bring to your attention.

Whether your conservatory is to be used as an extension to the house, or an extension of your garden, double glazing should be considered as an essential. The cost of heating a single glazed unit can frighten even the most wealthy. The optimum thickness for a sealed unit will leave you with a 16mm cavity within the glazed unit.

Heating requirements will be quite different from that of the house. You would be advised not to extend the central heating system as few systems have the capacity to reliably add another radiator. Heating is required typically late evening and very early in the morning which may conflict with the household requirements.

Low consumption electric wall heaters of the convection type are normally more than adequate and allow far greater control. For example, if a severe frost were expected this type of heater can be set to cut in at any time to prevent damage to your plants. Underfloor heating is another option, however this system provides even less control than a central heating system and can be inordinately expensive to run.

Some conservatories are offered with gas filled or low emissitivity sealed units. This is a type of glazing which offers increased heat retention over a conventional sealed unit and 39% improvement. Obviously in the winter time this can be of great benefit and in the case of a north facing location the extra cost would quickly be recovered in reduced fuel bills.

South facing conservatories would not require this type of insulation as the heat build-up may well give internal temperatures in excess of 120°F (50°C). Few plants can cope with this extreme and the conservatory would also become unbearable for the family.

Many complaints from existing conservatory owners stem from the lack of adequate ventilation, often despite their efforts at the time of purchase.

62

Fanlight windows are the most specified type of openings, ironically they are also the most inefficient at removing hot air. The very minimum opening for any conservatory are full height top hung windows, allowing for limitations of hinging these are available up to 1.4m drop. It must be borne in mind however that these will protrude into the garden at just the height for a small child to run into, so are not ideal for the average family. Full height 'Tilt and Turn' windows, available up to 2.1m drop do not suffer from this potential danger and are far more suitable in most circumstances. This type of opening is also far more efficient in forcing the movement of stale air and has the advantage of being reasonably secure should it be accidentally left open when the house is unoccupied. The best ventilation is supplied by vertical sliding (sash) windows as can be seen on many original Orangery designs, however a modern conservatory built with this type of window would be considerably dearer than it's conventional equivalent.

Ventilating the roof space is absolutely essential. Here again there are two main options. Conventional roof-lights provide good ventilation, but you must ensure however that the supplier does guarantee them to at least 'severe' weather rating standard. The roof-vent should allow you to either have a 'trickle of air', right through to 'fully open', as you require. Manual operation by a worm drive is the most common control method. Unless your conservatory has a very high roof you would be best advised to stay away from the electronic operation. Few if any electric systems will provide the same life-span as the rest of the conservatory and experience shows that many are just unreliable, needing constant adjustment and attention.

Wax cartridge vent openers are again more liable to problems than the worm drive and would be best avoided. It cannot be overstated that if your home is unoccupied during the day, roof-vents should never be left even partly open, they are extremely attractive to house-breakers, obviously anyone standing on the conservatory roof would have ideal leverage to rip the open vent from it's fixing.

If your home is going to be unoccupied for most of the day, a ridge vent is a far more suitable solution. Situated along the ridge bar of the roof, the vent can be left open to extract the warm air that gathers in the roof space, this air then exits underneath the crest and finials. Although this type of ventilation does not move the warm air as quickly as the roof vents it will provide adequate ventilation in all but the most extreme circumstances. Obviously with this design there is no compromise of security if it is left open when the house is unoccupied.

Ridge vents should always be designed to allow you to close them in colder weather. Lean-to conservatories cannot accommodate this type of design so a good alternative is to locate a solar controlled extractor vent within the sealed units on the elevations adjacent to the house wall. This positioning will allow them to draw warm air from the highest point of the roof.

Some conservatories will inevitably have to be built adjacent to a neighbour's property or on the garden boundary line. In most cases the only solution offered is to build a brick side wall in order to provide privacy. Unfortunately this often cuts the amount of light transmitted to the existing house and compromises the growth of the plants that you intend to keep. The solution to both of these requirements is to build that side of the conservatory in the same framing you have specified for the rest of the structure, but instead of using double glazing in these panels, use insulated panels (available in various finishes) externally and safety glazed mirrors internally. The mirrors can be clear or slightly tinted if you suffer from reflected glare. In many cases this will provide more indirect lighting for the house than was available before and in north facing rooms, the benefit is quite dramatic, providing very even light for plant growth. A side benefit to this design is the incredible feel of space given to the conservatory.

Many conservatories are built with a dwarf brick wall, typically 0.45-0.6m high. This design gives the advantage of an internal window ledge, ideal for pot plants. Thought should be given to the internal finish of this wall from an early stage. Often an internal plaster finish is chosen as a means of making the conservatory feel more room-like, this will also give a smooth finish, it has a safety factor, as young children can be grazed against a face-brick finish, should they fall against it. The plaster finish may have disadvantages though, if you are keeping plants in your conservatory that require high humidity levels, as plaster will always readily absorb water and become damp, leading to the growth of mildew and black mould. Once this has been allowed to develop the only sure way to be rid of the problem is to replace all the affected plaster, with the inevitable expense. With prior planning this irritation can be avoided.

Prepare for all of the apparently conflicting advice you may be given, by making a list of your specific requirements and when you start to get quotations make sure everything you require is included, that way you can more readily make comparisons. If the total exceeds your budget you may have to make sacrifices from your list. Never place an order with a company who cannot do the complete installation. Any

64

work that is sub-contracted is open to dispute in the event of problems and you will not be able to get recompense. Always ask to meet an existing client of your supplier to verify their standard of work and customer satisfaction. A display conservatory may look perfect, but how does it look after a year or two?

When you start to gather your quotations, you should see a pattern emerge of similar prices, but you may find one price that is much lower than the others. This is almost certainly a compromise on quality and you should not be tempted. Source your quotes from National and Local companies. Check how long the company has been in business and if they belong to the Glass and Glazing Federation, (GGF). Members of the GGF will have a proven trading history and a deposit indemnity. It was the GGF who pushed for legislation to ensure 'safety glass' is now used in all conservatories.

Properly planned is trouble free, and once you have your conservatory installed it will become the focal point of your home. You will wonder how you ever managed without it and what ever size it is, you will wish you had made it larger. There is nothing to match the pleasure of sitting in your conservatory on Christmas Day, picking a fresh orange from the tree and adding a slice of fresh picked lemon to your favourite drink.

Citrus Varieties To Grow And Enjoy

CHOOSING YOUR CITRUS TREE

The varieties chosen for this book are the varieties you would normally see, or have in recent years seen in European shops. They have been developed for their flavour, texture and consumer appeal. Varieties fall in and out of popularity very quickly and are regularly superseded by better or improved strains. It does not set out to be a comprehensive list of citrus fruits. Many of the old varieties you may have eaten when young are no longer grown, or if they are grown, they would be for the farmer's own use and not marketed.

We would normally be able to supply all the trees mentioned, but if they lose their consumer appeal, then availability of the trees themselves would be withdrawn due to lack of production. Some of the varieties shown would not be suitable for our temperate climate, as they dislike rain on their leaves, but they are included to show the differences and also for those who may already grow them but wonder why they are having problems with the resulting fruit drop.

Varieties of citrus fruits can be categorized into different groups, each group being identified by certain characteristics that are common or similar to others in it's group.

The first to be discussed are the Mandarins. This is a collective name which includes Satsumas, Clementines, Tangors, Tangelos, and other Hybrids commonly called 'Mandarins'. Some people refer to Mandarins as 'Tangerines'. It may be better to just refer to varieties in this group by name and then we all know what we are talking about.

If you are limited for space but prefer to keep a tree that produces a lot of fruit and one that can be kept trimmed back as a small bush, then the Clementines may be the best for you. Large fruits look better on larger trees and those trees with open habit require more room to look effective and produce a good crop.

The characteristics of the Satsuma are that they are generally very easy to peel with a loose skin and their shape is rather flattened at the top and bottom. These fruits can be quite large, we have actually grown them to be almost the size of a hand. Satsumas also tend to have a more open habit and can quickly develop a weeping shape with long branches supporting a heavy weight of fruit. Satsumas should always be seedless.

Clementines are the smaller of the Mandarin family, although not difficult to peel, the skin is not as puffy as on the Satsuma and tends to be quite thin. The shape is round rather than flattened, and they can often have a more distinctive aroma than satsumas. Some of the Clementines have a deep orange, almost red colour and look very attractive on the tree.

Spain is the only country to have developed true seedless varieties of Clementines. Some only remain seedless if grown in isolation, others will revert to becoming seedy if cross pollinated with other varieties. This point should be borne in mind when growing different varieties of Clementines in close proximity, such as in a conservatory or on the patio. If you want to grow more than one variety then choose only those that will not revert.

The fruits we would commonly refer to as 'Mandarins' are those that are characterized by having an acid to sugar ratio that gives the fruit a 'bite', in other words, they are rather more acid than the sweet satsumas or clementines.

The acidity levels may drop in some fruits, if they are left on the tree a little longer, but as most of these varieties are seedy, coupled with their acidity levels, they are losing favour. Mandarins Nova and Fortune are the new varieties in this group and will remain seedless if not pollinated. Mandarins are generally smaller than satsumas but larger than clementines and are not as easy to peel as the satsumas.

We normally stock only five Navel varieties which we will bring to your attention, they are the ones you would be most familiar with. The name derives from the well developed navel which is generally visible externally, but is seen internally as a smaller fruit, contained within the base of the main fruit. They are harvested at two-weekly intervals, between varieties, but as navels can remain on the tree in good commercial condition for some time, there may be some considerable overlap between the varieties appearing in the shops.

Navel oranges should not be used for juicing if the juice is to stand for any time, as the fruit will produce an after bitter taste due to the presence of a chemical known as *limonin.* This is only present at very low levels, but as the intensity of the bitterness is quite strong it can be detected by most people. It can be mixed with other juices with lower levels of limonin if required. This would mainly be the fruits from the Blanco (sweet) varieties or the Pigmented varieties.

Not many shops at present label oranges as a particular variety, a general description of 'Navel' may be all that you will see, but this label may cover at least a dozen varieties each with subtle differences in flavour, texture, juice content and acidity. When you know the difference, you will know what to look for and what would appeal to you most, so insist on proper identification.

Blanco oranges are also referred to as sweet varieties as they generally contain less acidity and a lower level of the chemical limonin. Some have such a low acid level that they become rather insipid in taste. These oranges are sometimes referred to as 'sugar' oranges and are favoured in some Arab countries.

Blanco oranges are the ones used extensively in fruit juice manufacture as they generally have a larger juice content which is of high quality. They are not all seedless.

Pigmented oranges are also referred to as 'Blood' oranges because of their red-pigmentation. They are thought to have originated in the Mediterranean regions.

Blood oranges have many similar characteristics with Blanco oranges, but they contain red pigments known as *anthocyanins*, which although present in many plant tissues such as leaves and flowers, develop in the flesh, the juice and sometimes the rind of blood oranges in low night temperatures in the autumn and winter. In tropical and semi-tropical climates, the pigmentation does not develop, but there may be some flecks of colour which develop after harvest, when the fruit is stored.

The variations of pigmentation are considerable, from slight colour changes to a deep purple. The fruits grown in shadier conditions within the tree canopy or on the shadier side of the tree may have the strongest colour changes. The flavour may also be changed by these variations, the stronger the colour the more the fruit tastes similar to raspberries or cherries.

Production limitations and the tendency to produce small fruits as well as the popularity of the navels, has meant that the Blood oranges gradually lost favour with the consumer, although they are still grown in small pockets mainly for the farmer's own use.

Juice from the pigmented oranges is best made and used fresh. It has a very distinctive colour, flavour and aroma, but if left, the colour may change and look unpalatable.

Pre-packed processed juice from the blood oranges is now available to the consumer. If this pigmented juice becomes popular then there may be more pigmented varieties of fruit available in the shops as well.

Sour oranges are both sour and bitter due to the high levels of acid and the presence of the bitter compound *neo-hesperidin*. For many years they have been used as a root stock on which other varieties have been grown. It was popular for this purpose because of it's ability to withstand adverse environmental conditions better than other varieties and because of it's tolerance to the cold. The use of sour orange for this purpose has now been banned in Spain due to it's susceptibility to virus diseases.

Sour orange is grown from seed because it is an original variety and not a hybrid. It makes a handsome specimen tree with an upright growth habit although very thorny, and is often used as an attractive decorative tree lining the streets to provide shade in Mediterranean countries. They cause dismay to the visitors who feel the excitement of picking oranges only to be disillusioned when they get the fruit to their hotel room.

These trees are very productive, the flowers are used extensively in the perfume industry and the fruit which hangs on the tree with deep reddish-orange colour is used in the production of marmalade. Extracts from the fruit are also used for flavouring soft drinks and liqueurs such as Cointreau and Curacao.

In some countries the local people pay for the privilege of collecting the flowers for processing into essential oils, when the trees are in blossom in March and April.

A favourite in the UK is the Calamondin orange, grown as a house plant, and kept to minimal size. The appeal for this variety is that it produces blossom and fruit all year round. It is kept for decoration rather than for it's fruit, although the fruit will make excellent marmalade, or can be pickled in brandy or used in recipes flavoured by oranges. The fruits are very small and are quite seedy. It is preferable to remove the ripe fruits after you have enjoyed the visual effect for a while, store them in the freezer and when you have collected sufficient you can process them.

Calamondin orange has sometimes been used as root-stock, and may be produced from seeds or cuttings.

With all orange, and mandarin varieties, the fruit should not be left on the tree for longer than the recommended time, or the tree starts to feed from the fruit instead of feeding from the roots. This has the effect of drying out the fruit which then becomes unpalatable. The tree suffers from the lack of food and the new blossom will not appear. Always remove ripe fruit before the spring blossom is due.

The origin of the Grapefruit is uncertain but it is thought to be a cross between a sweet orange and a Shaddock (pummelo), but it may be the way the fruit hangs in bunches that gave rise to the inclusion of 'Grape' in the name. The first records that mention 'Grapefruit' were in 1823 and it was given the species name of *Citrus paradisi* in 1830 after the local name 'forbidden fruit'.

Grapefruits in general prefer warmer and more humid climates in order to produce good quality fruit and may be planted inside a conservatory or Orangery providing the humidity levels are kept quite high. In the cooler drier Mediterranean climates there is a tendency for the fruit to have a thicker rind, have higher acid levels and to have some bitterness. In some countries grapefruits are considered to be the 'poor man's orange'. The root-stock, as with most citrus production is very influential in the quality of the fruit.

Grapefruit can be divided into two groups, the common or white, in which Marsh is the most significant, and the pigmented varieties which have numerous names. Some fruits have less pigmentation and others have a deeper red colour. These have a tendency to be sweeter and have become extremely popular. Florida with it's hot and humid climate, has become the world's leading producer of grapefruits.

The chemical responsible for the pigmentation in grapefruit is *lycopene*. This is activated by prolonged high temperatures and not the cold, as in the pigmentation of blood oranges.

Grapefruit seeds are often planted in the UK as they are frequently found to be germinating inside the fruit when it is cut open for eating. Keen gardeners cannot resist the temptation to plant the seeds in this condition. No guarantee is given that these seeds will grow to produce fruit, although many do have success. The fruit is generally of poor quality because of the lack of root-stock. Good feeding may help to improve the quality of these fruits.

72

A selection of Citrus Trees available at Global Orange Groves UK

Cultivation of limes is being considered in Spain and experiments are being made with different types of root-stock. When grown on sour orange it has more resistance to cold and adverse ground conditions, but is susceptible to virus, such a *Tristeza*. When grown on Carrizo, which is favoured because of it's disease resistance, the fruit tends to drop prematurely, however this can be treated with chemicals.

Lime trees along with the grapefruits will tolerate being planted inside a conservatory or Orangery provided the humidity level is kept quite high.

Lemons are very popular with the amateur gardener because most varieties seem to be continuously in flower and fruit. The fruits themselves are used extensively in the kitchen to flavour food and drinks and to have one's own supply at hand to pick fresh as required, is wonderful.

Lemons are thought to have originated in India and then brought to the Mediterranean in the 12th Century. They are not grown very much in the tropics because in the humid conditions lemons are more susceptible to pests and diseases. Limes are an adequate substitute and far more suited to high humidity levels.

Lemon trees are vigorous in their growth but are more cold sensitive than other varieties of citrus. The fruits vary in their acid levels and in their juice content. Some varieties of lemon are more prolific fruiters than others and you will often find lemons at all stages of development, with differences in the shape of the fruit and the thickness of the skin, all on the same tree.

Commercially harvested lemons are normally held in cold storage for long periods after harvest in order to spread the availability in the market. This sometimes affects the quality of the fruit. The summer crop of lemons is sometimes called the 'verdi' crop because without the low temperatures, the colour does not always fully develop. This crop is not as well marketed.

Kumquats are related to citrus but have their own genus *Fortunella*. It is thought they are more tolerant of indoor dry atmospheres than many other varieties.

To regulate the size and height of your tree, regular pruning will be needed. These are agricultural trees that will grow quite large if not controlled in this way.

74

SATSUMA OWARI

citrus unshiu

The satsuma owari tree is vigorous but with a rather open habit. The tree will often produce very long branches that will hang low with the weight of fruit and makes an excellent 'weeping' shape. This variety originated in Japan but was imported into Spain around 1925.

It is very productive with fruits that are large but flattened in shape. The flavour is sweet and the fruit has a high quantity of good quality juice. It is always seedless. The fruit can be picked in October and should generally be harvested by Christmas. The skin will become loose and puffy if the fruit is left on the tree too long. At this stage it may well have started to dry out with the resulting loss of juice and flavour. It is easy to peel and appeals well to children.

SATSUMA OKITSU

okitsu wase

Satsuma Okitsu, as the name suggests, is a Japanese variety. It is a relatively recent introduction to Spain but is becoming popular due to it's excellent sweet flavour.

The tree is small with a more bushy habit, not as open as the Owari, with leaves that are a less intense green. The fruit is seedless and a good size, the shape being typical satsuma, slightly flattened, and it has a high quantity of good quality juice. The harvest is early in October.

SATSUMA CLAUSELLINA

The Satsuma Clausellina is a variety that was formed by a bud mutation from the Owari and was found in Almazora, Castellon de la Plana in 1962. The tree is not as vigorous as the Satsuma Owari, it has smaller leaves and a more bushy habit.

The fruit is smaller with a high quantity of juice of an inferior quality, the fruit although not as sweet as the Owari, is seedless.

The tree is very productive even in drought conditions. The fruit is generally available in the shops about three weeks before the Owari and is therefore one of the earliest available Spanish satsumas, appearing early in October.

SATSUMA OWARI

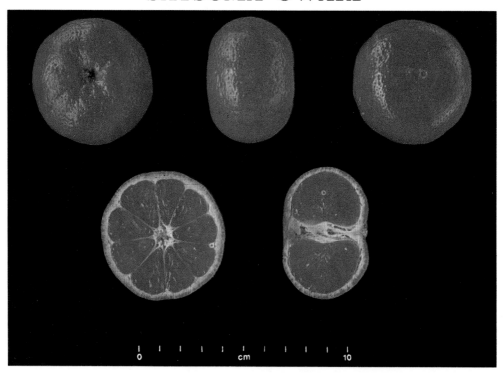

SATSUMA CLAUSELLINA

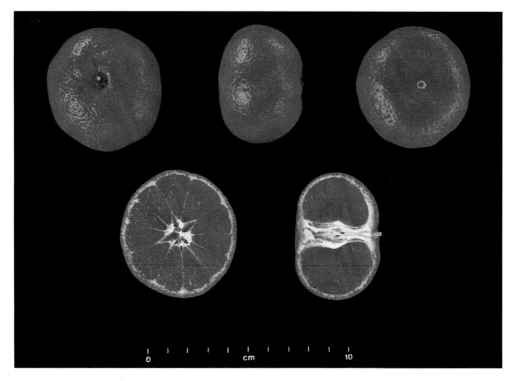

CLEMENTINE FINA

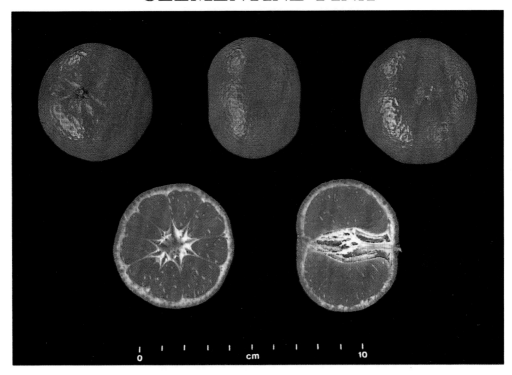

CLEMENTINE OROVAL

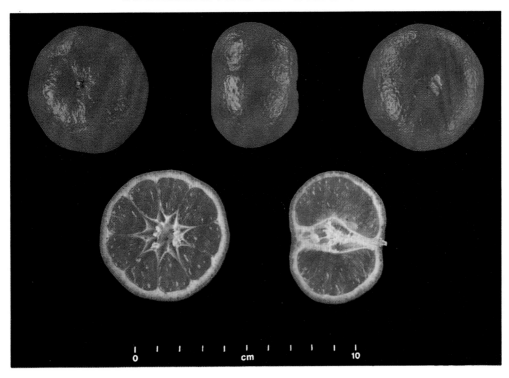

CLEMENTINE FINA

citrus reticulata

This variety is also known as the Seedless Clementine, and Clementina del Terreno. It might well be called the 'father' of all clementines, as so many other varieties have resulted from this tree.

The tree is vigorous, large and very bushy. It produces a large crop of small round fruits which have the distinctive aroma that has become associated with clementines.

The seedless fruits are early ripening, but can be left on the tree in good condition for some time.

CLEMENTINE OROVAL

This variety originated as a spontaneous mutation of the Fina and was found in Quart de les Valls in Valencia in 1950.

Although in early years the tree tends to be thorny, this condition disappears with age.

The tree is vigorous and very productive, producing large, very juicy, slightly acid fruits that are seedless.

This is an early maturing variety which can be harvested before the Fina, but it will not stay on the tree for very long and retain it's condition.

After a period of heavy rain or dew the tree is liable to shed it's fruit, so extra protection against the rain will be necessary for it to be grown in the UK.

CLEMENTINE DE NULES

This variety is also known as Clemenules and was first discovered near the town of Nules in Castellon Province as a bud mutation on a Fina tree. It can be grown and kept as a small bush as the leaves are smaller than most other fruits and the foliage is quite dense.

It is the most popular variety grown in Spain. It is vigorous and very productive with good sized fruit containing a high quantity of high quality juice. It is seedless.

The tree will often produce more than one crop of fruit, although the size and quality of the fruit may vary between each fruit set. The fruit can be harvested after November and up to the end of January as the fruit quality remains good while the fruit is on the tree.

CLEMENTINE TOMATERA

This variety originated from a spontaneous mutation of the Fina and Burriana in Castellon de la Plana.

The tree is vigorous, reaching a good size with very red medium sized seedless fruit, larger than the Fina and smaller than the Clemenules, but containing a high quantity of juice. The tree does have some thorns in the early years.

The fruit can be harvested after November. The skin colour is a deep orange almost red colour, hence the name 'Tomatera' or 'tomato coloured'.

To ensure that this tree remains seedless, it should not be grown with other mandarin varieties.

Tomatera is already losing favour in the market place and availability is not guaranteed.

CLEMENTINE DE NULES

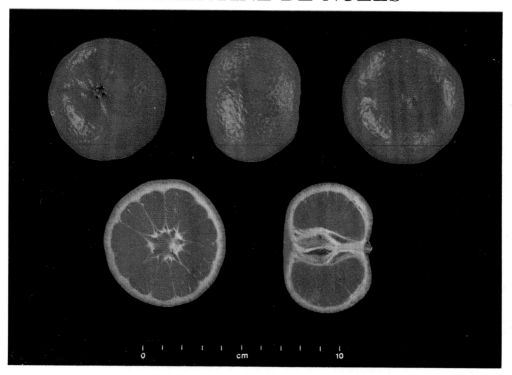

CLEMENTINE TOMATERA

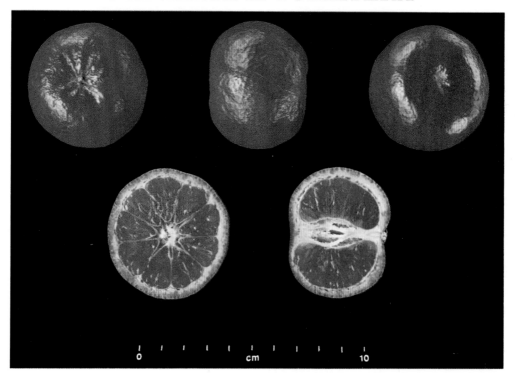

CLEMENTINE ESBAL

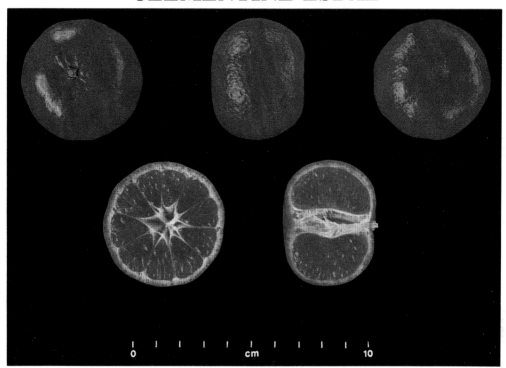

CLEMENTINE HERNANDINA

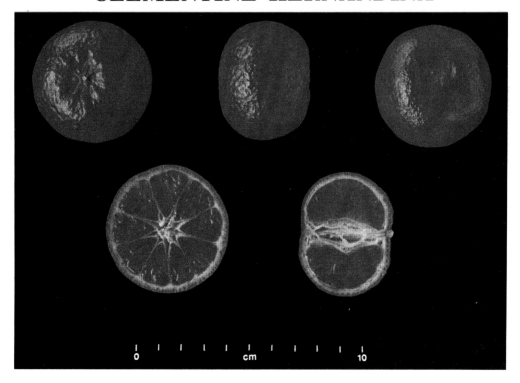

81

CLEMENTINE ESBAL

Fina again produced a spontaneous mutation, this one found in Sagunto, Valencia in 1966.

The tree is vigorous and grows to a good size, with fruits that are slightly larger than the Clementine Fina, although still considered to be a small fruit.

The fruit has an excellent flavour and is seedless, maturing early before the Fina, but it will not hang on the tree in good condition and will be damaged by rain and dew, so would not be a suitable tree to grow in England on the patio, it would need constant protection from the weather.

CLEMENTINE HERNANDINA

Yet another spontaneous mutation from the Fina, also found in 1966, this time in Picasent, Valencia.

Again the tree is vigorous and the fruit is similar to the Fina but the full colour of the rind does not develop until 2 months after the Fina.

Harvest is generally about the middle of February to March, and the colour of the fruit may not be completely developed even then, although internally the fruit is more mature than skin colour would indicate.

This variety will not hang well on the tree after maturity as the fruits will have a tendency to shrink and deteriorate.

CLEMENTINE CLEMENTARD

The origin of this variety is unknown, but it is thought to have come from the Fina like many other varieties.

It is much like the Hernandina, the only difference being that the colour is less intense and the colour change is later than the Hernandina.

CLEMENTINE MARISOL

This spontaneous mutation was from the Clementine Oroval and was found in 1970 at Bechi in Castellon de la Plana, Spain.

The characteristics are the same as the Oroval, producing large slightly acid, seedless, but juicy fruits.

The difference is that the Marisol can be harvested 2 weeks before the Oroval.

This variety may also have a tendency to shed it's fruit after heavy rain.

CLEMENTINE CLEMENTARD

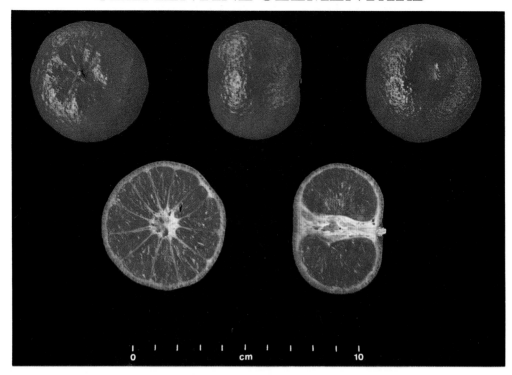

CLEMENTINE MARISOL

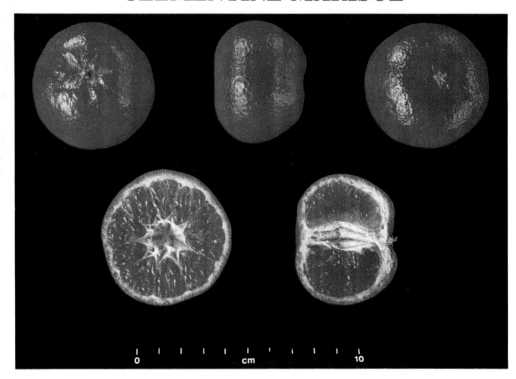

CLEMENTINE ARRUFATINA

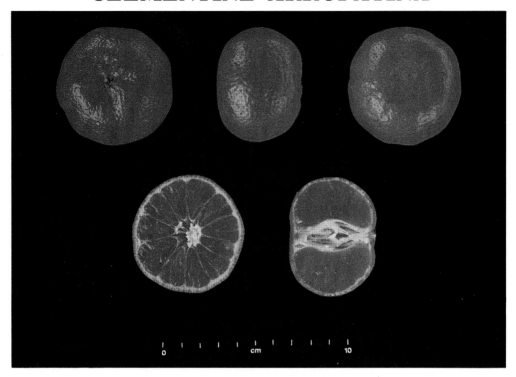

MANDARIN COMUN

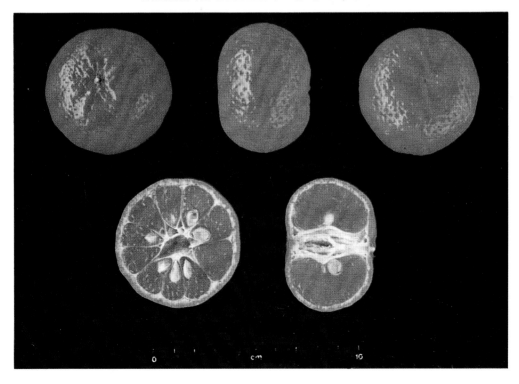

CLEMENTINE ARRUFATINA

Another spontaneous mutation, this time found on a Clementine de Nules, at Villarreal in Castellon de Plana, Spain in 1968.

This variety is vigorous and will grow quite large, but may have thorns in the early years. These seem to disappear as the tree matures.

It is very productive, producing seedless fruits of relatively good quality.

The fruits should be harvested as soon as the colour starts to develop as the fruit will dry up if left on the tree too long.

MANDARIN COMUN

citrus reticulata

This origin of this variety is unknown, it has been grown for a long time, hence the name 'Common Mandarin'.

It is vigorous, with smaller leaves than some of the others but is very productive, producing good sized fruit, larger than clementines and smaller than satsumas. It has an adequate quantity of juice but produces quite a lot of seeds. This makes it less popular than other newer varieties.

The fruit can be collected after December, but will lose it's quality if left on the tree too long.

MANDARIN FORTUNE

The Fortune is a hybrid of the Fina and the Dancy and was produced by J R Furr in California in 1964. It is more popular in Spain than in other countries and grows well there.

The tree is vigorous, reaching a good size. The medium size fruit is of good quality and has a high quantity of juice which may be slightly acid to the taste.

This is a late variety and the harvest is March. If too acid when the first sample is picked, acidity will reduce if remaining fruits are left a little longer on the tree. It is considered to have good consumer appeal.

To ensure the tree remains seedless, it should not be grown with other mandarin varieties.

MANDARIN KARA

In California, in 1915, H B Frost produced this variety by crossing a Satsuma Owari with a King Mandarin.

It has similar characteristics to the Satsuma, and is moderately vigorous, with a more open habit than the Clementine varieties and the branches have a tendency to droop.

The fruit is of a good size but is rather seedy, which is not very popular with the consumer, and the flavour is noticeably acid, reducing it's market appeal still further.

The fruit is harvested after March when the colour is deep orange.

MANDARIN FORTUNE

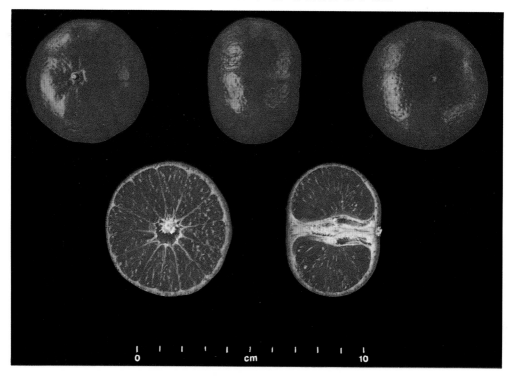

MANDARIN KARA

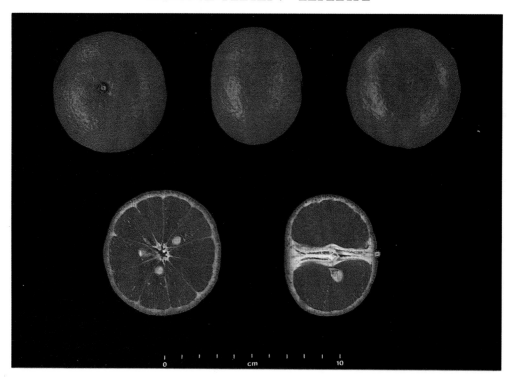

MANDARIN NOVA

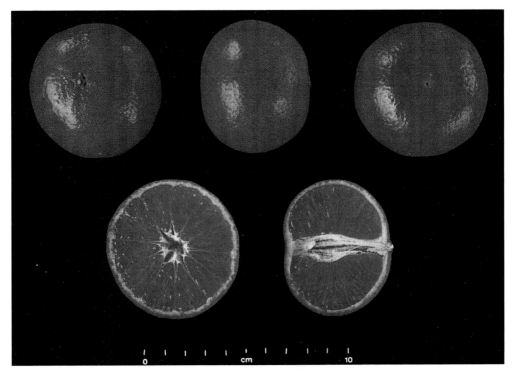

MANDARIN WILKING

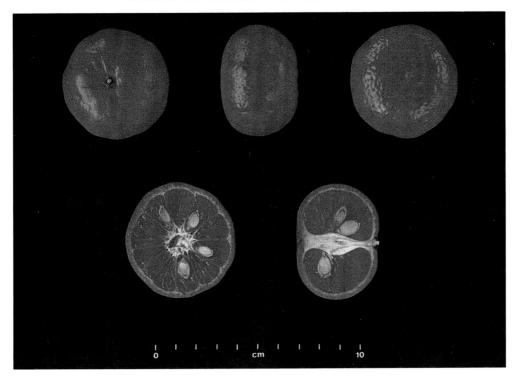

MANDARIN NOVA

Clemenvilla is another name for this variety. It is a cross between the Fina and the Orlando, produced by Gardner and Bellows in Florida in 1942.

The tree is vigorous, reaching a good size and the fruit is medium to large for a mandarin, and is generally seedless. This is a sweet juicy variety which peels easily and cleanly, the colour is excellent being reddish-orange.

Harvest is after December, but the fruit should not be left on the tree too long as the quality will deteriorate and the skin itself may start to split.

This variety should be grown in isolation from other mandarin varieties to ensure it remains seedless.

MANDARIN WILKING

This variety is another cross with the King Mandarin, but this time with a Mandarin Comun, again by H B Frost in 1915.

The tree is moderately vigorous but not reliable in it's harvest. It may produce very little, or may be so heavily laden it loses all it's strength.

The fruits are very seedy, shaped more like the Satsumas, and have a good flavour, but have become less marketable with so many seedless varieties now available.

THE SWEET ORANGES

citrus sinensis

WASHINGTON NAVEL ORANGE

The origin of this variety is not certain but is thought to be a spontaneous mutation found in Bahia, Brazil in the late 1800's.

This tree is vigorous and the fruit is very large and seedless. Washington Navels are generally considered to have the best flavour of all the navel oranges.

The fruit contains a good quantity of juice and will stay on the tree for quite a long time in good commercial condition. It would normally be harvested in November.

The tree does produce large thorns, and when compared with the Navelina for growing at home, this gives it second place.

THOMSON NAVEL ORANGE

This was one of the first spontaneous mutations from the Washington Navel, found in California by A C Thomson in 1891.

The tree is not as vigorous as the Washington, and does not grow as large, but it is very productive. The fruit is comparable in size, is also seedless and is ready for harvest 2 weeks before the Washington, but it lacks the quality and so other, better oranges have overridden this particular variety in popularity and consumer appeal.

WASHINGTON NAVEL ORANGE

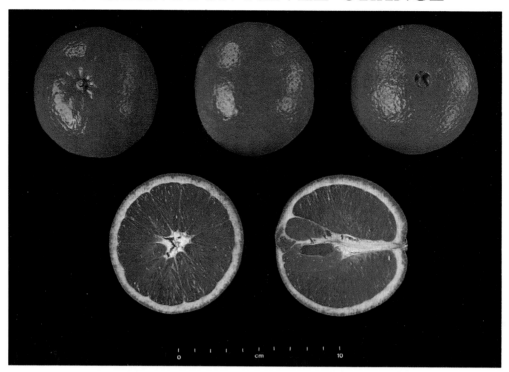

THOMSON NAVEL ORANGE

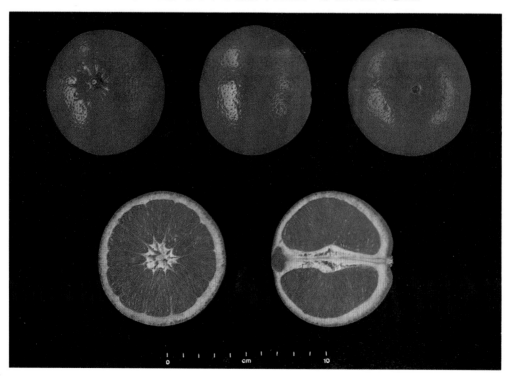

NAVELINA ORANGE

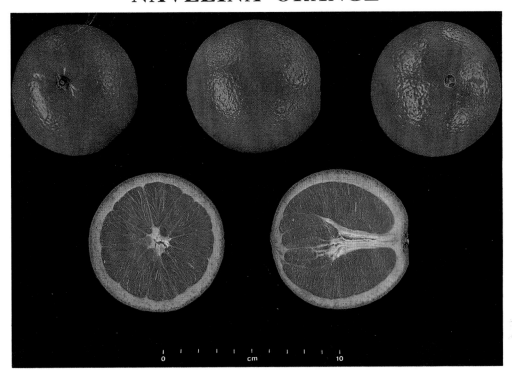

NEWHALL NAVEL ORANGE

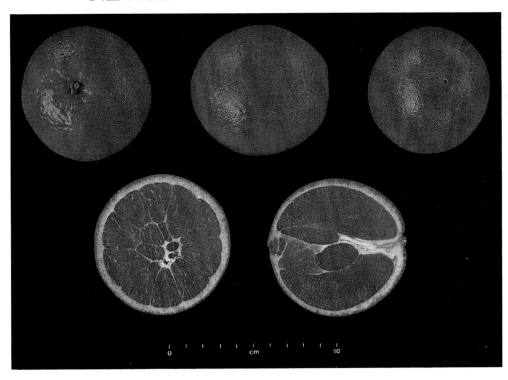

93

NAVELINA ORANGE

The origin of this variety is not well known, but it is thought to have originated in California, it is now considered to be basically a Spanish variety, as it is grown there extensively.

This variety is vigorous, but the tree is classed as being a small to medium size when mature. It produces large seedless fruit, similar to the Washington, but a little smaller and more oval in shape, containing a navel.

The quality is excellent, the fruit contains a good quantity of juice, and the fruit can be harvested in the third week of October, which is before the Washington Navel.

The Navelinas are very popular with consumers and as the tree does not have thorns like the Washington Navel, it is often preferred by the amateur gardener.

NEWHALL NAVEL ORANGE

The Newhall is again of Californian origin, possibly a mutation from the Navelina.

It is almost indistinguishable from the Navelina in size, shape and texture and is in fact marketed with the Navelina, no distinction being made between them, but the juice of the Newhall has less acidity.

The tree characteristics are the same as the Navelina, but the Newhall may have thorns. The harvest is two weeks before, and this must therefore be the earliest of the Navels on the consumer market.

NAVELATE ORANGE

The origin of this variety is Spanish, having been found as a spontaneous mutation on a Washington Navel, by D A Gil at Vinaroz, Castellon Province, in 1948.

The trees are vigorous and can grow to a large size, but they have some thorns.

The fruit is medium to large and slightly inferior to the Washington. It has the usual navel, but this may not be as visible externally as on the Washington Navel.

The tree is not very productive but the fruit will stay on the tree for a few months in perfect condition. The external colour of the fruit is later developing than the Washington Navel, but the fruit can be harvested before full colour develops, as internally the fruit will be ripe.

Harvest is generally after November, and it is the last of the Navels to be harvested, hence the name 'Navel-late'.

BLANCO ORANGES

COMUNA ORANGE

The origin of this variety is unknown, but the tree is vigorous and reaches a good size.

The fruit is medium to large with a large quantity of juice. The serious disadvantage is the number of seeds this variety has. Harvest is mid-season, after December, and although the tree is very productive, with so many other varieties of better quality and consumer appeal, few of these trees are planted.

NAVELATE ORANGE

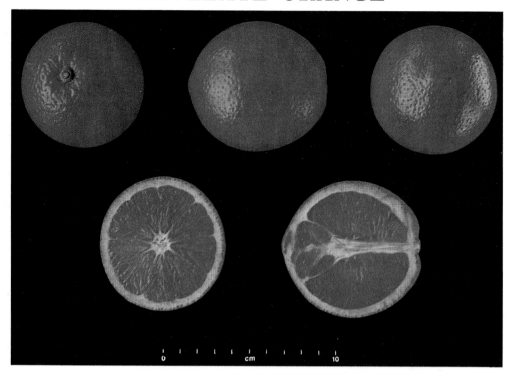

COMUNA ORANGE

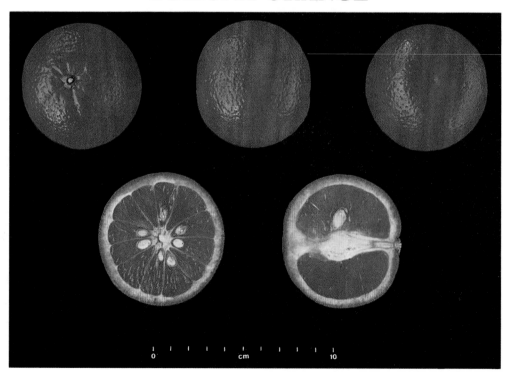

CADENERA ORANGE

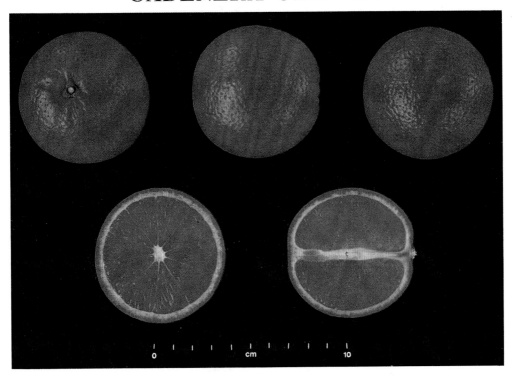

SALUSTIANA ORANGE

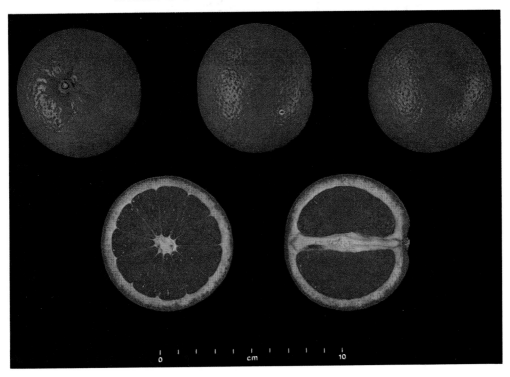

97

CADENERA ORANGE

This is a Spanish variety the origin of which is uncertain, but it is thought to have originated from the Comuna. It has been known since 1870.

The trees are vigorous and reach a good size, with fruit that is medium to large. The juice content is good and of excellent quality.

The fruit is almost seedless with a fairly rich flavour and can stay on the tree in good commercial condition for a long time after the expected harvest in November.

It was once the most popular orange grown in Spain, but since the introduction of the Navel oranges, it's popularity has reduced.

SALUSTIANA ORANGE

This is a seedless variety of the Comuna orange, found as a spontaneous mutation, by Don Salustiano Pallas near Enovo, in the province of Valencia in 1950.

It is a vigorous, good sized tree and very productive, with medium sized, very juicy, high quality oranges which are very sweet. The flesh is smooth in texture and the internal characteristics are very distinctive in their appearance.

The fruit is usually seedless and will stay on the tree for a long time in good condition. The fruits can be harvested after November, but are at their best if left a little longer on the tree.

This variety is the most important mid-season orange in the group of Blancas and they are being planted extensively in Spain.

These trees will produce very large thorns, but for the purpose of a home grown tree in the conservatory or on the patio, these thorns can easily be cut off, and should not deter the purchaser if the fruit is of interest.

CASTELLANA ORANGE

A Spanish variety, of unknown origin, but vigorous and productive.

The fruits are medium to large and fairly seedy, but the juice content and quality is good.

Harvest is after November, but the fruit can stay on the tree long after harvest time, in good commercial condition.

The seediness of this variety is a serious limitation to it's commercial importance and production.

BERNA ORANGE

The Berna, sometimes called Verna (not to be confused with the Verna lemon) is also a Spanish variety of unknown origin. It is vigorous and grows to a medium height.

The fruits are oval in shape, small to medium in size and most fruits are seedless, but with less juice than other varieties.

The Berna is not ready for harvest until the end of March making this a late variety. It can be left on the tree but with the rise in temperature, the colour changes back to green.

Although the tree is very productive, the flavour and sweetness of the fruit cannot compare with the Valencia Late which is ready about the same time, so it is lacking commercial appeal.

CASTELLANA ORANGE

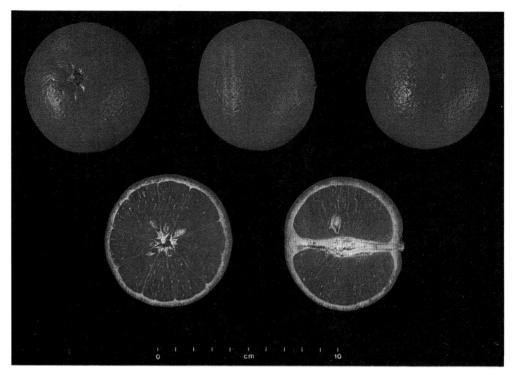

BERNA ORANGE

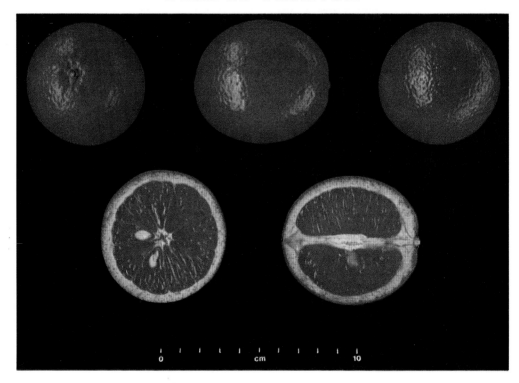

VALENCIA LATE ORANGE

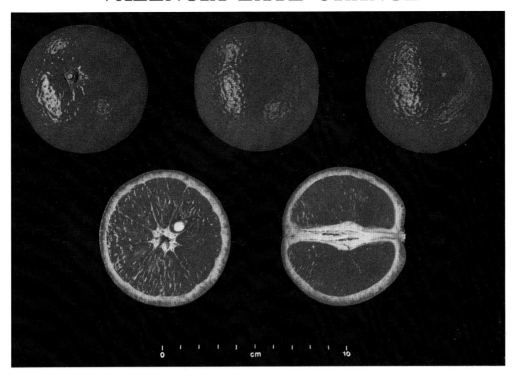

DOBLE FINA

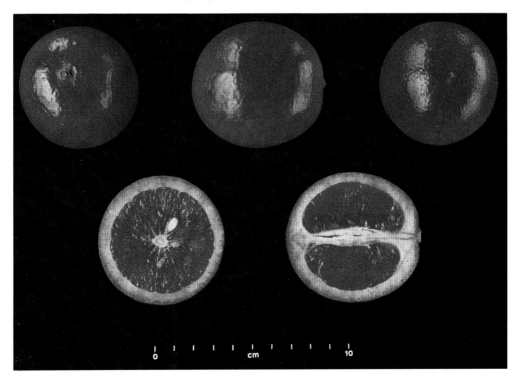

101

VALENCIA LATE ORANGE

This variety is the most important orange variety for all citrus growing countries of the world. It is used extensively in processing to juice as it does not produce an after bitter taste like other varieties, such as Navels. It has a high juice content that is of excellent flavour, colour and sweetness, any acidity disappears with maturity.

The tree is vigorous, shapes beautifully for a container grown tree, and the medium to large fruits do contain some seeds, but not many, usually about two to four per fruit.

Valencia oranges are harvested after March, being the last of the late varieties, hence the name 'Valencia Late'. The fruit will stay on the tree for a few months in good condition but because of the rise in summer temperatures, the skin colour will revert to green. Commercially this is rectified by reducing temperatures during storage.

This tree will need to be well fed to prevent it reducing it's crop size for the second, or alternate year. In ideal conditions and with good feeding we have this tree producing a second flush of blossom late in the season.

PIGMENTED ORANGES

DOBLE FINA

This variety is also known as Oval Sangre, Sanguina Oval and Rojo Oval. It's origin is unknown, but the tree is vigorous and grows to a good size.

The fruit is medium sized, almost seedless and with adequate juice, but the quality varies with the district in which it is grown. This then assumes, soil quality, pH, or climatic conditions will affect the fruit, so be sure to feed adequately if growing this tree.

The colour or pigmentation of the fruit is in correlation to the blush of the skin, therefore indicating how intense the internal colour is. The fruit has a distinctive blood-orange flavour. The tree is very productive, harvest is after January, but the fruit has a tendency to drop and therefore this variety is unreliable and has only a small localised commercial interest.

ENTREFINA

This variety is also known as Inglesa, meaning English, although the reason for this is not known. It was found as a spontaneous mutation on the Doble Fina in Castellon de Plana, Spain.

The variety takes on the characteristics of the Doble Fina, with medium sized, almost seedless fruit with pigment variations, and with the blood orange flavour, although the skin is smoother than the Doble Fina.

The tree is very productive, harvest is after January, the same as the Doble Fina, but the fruit also has a tendency to drop prematurely.

SANGUINELLI ORANGE

This is another spontaneous mutation from the Doble Fina, found in 1929 in Almenara, Castellon de la Plana, Spain.

The tree is vigorous and attains a good size, but is thornless.

The fruit is oval in shape, medium size and the skin has a reddish pigment. The flesh also has a reddish colour and in some cases deep red. It does have some seeds.

There is a high quantity of good quality juice, sweeter and less acidic than the Doble Fina.

The Sanguinelli is very productive and can be harvested after January. The fruit hangs better on the tree than other pigmented oranges, but it's commercial appeal has been greatly diminished in favour of other citrus varieties.

ENTREFINA

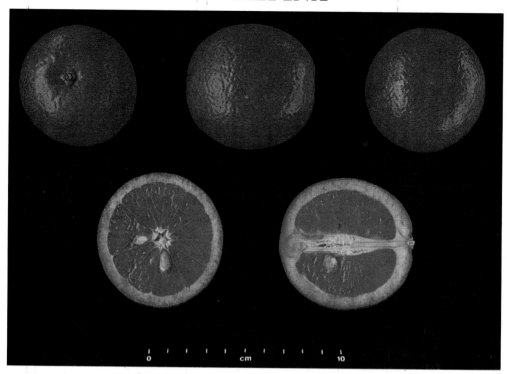

SANGUINELLI ORANGE

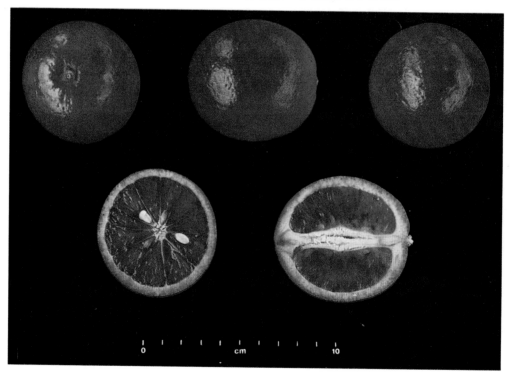

NARANJA AMARGA

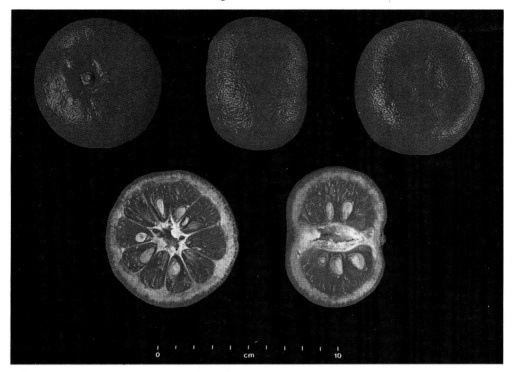

BEARS LIME

105

Sour Or Bitter Oranges

citrus aurantium

NARANJA AMARGA

This variety is also known as Naranja Agria, and Seville Marmalade Orange. It is one of the few varieties cultivated from seed. The tree is vigorous, reaches a good height and is very productive.

The fruit is of medium size, slightly flattened in shape and has many seeds. The flavour is very bitter and acidic and this fruit cannot be eaten fresh. It is generally harvested for processing into marmalade, but is also used for the production of essential oils used in the manufacture of perfumes. Oil of Petitgrain is distilled from the crushed leaves and oil of Neroli from the flowers.

The harvest is generally after January, but with less marmalade being produced at the present time, their commercial appeal is declining.

Lime

BEARS LIME

citrus latifolia

Also known as Persian and Tahiti Lime although no longer grown in either country. It is thought to have originated in 1850, possibly grown from a seed of the original Tahiti Lime. The tree is very compact with a few small thorns. It is very productive.

The fruit is larger than the Mexican Lime and is seedless containing about 45% juice. Skin colour is dark green but will change to yellow if left on the tree past harvest.

106

GRAPEFRUITS

citrus paradisi

WHITE MARSH GRAPEFRUIT

White Marsh is also known as Marsh Seedless and originated as a seedling from a Duncan tree in Florida about 1860. It is not completely seedless as it's name may suggest, but generally has two or three seeds per fruit. The tree has taken on the characteristics of the Duncan, being vigorous and very productive. The fruit is sweet, particularly if not picked too soon, as the acidity level drops when the fruit is left on the tree. If the acidity levels drops too low, the flavour becomes insipid. The fruit can be harvested after October.

This variety is the most common variety grown world wide, but in Florida the pigmented varieties are gaining ground in popularity.

The White Marsh is used extensively in the processing industry for juicing, the segments are also used because they retain their stability during processing.

REDBLUSH GRAPEFRUIT

This variety is also known as Ruby, Ruby Red, Red Marsh and Red Seedless. There may be subtle differences between the names, but they are generally considered to be the same. It originated in Texas and was discovered by A E Henninger as a bud mutation of the variety known as Thompson, in 1931.

The tree is very vigorous and will become quite large, so needs to be cut back to keep it in check when grown in a container. The tree may produce some thorns.

The fruit has a thick skin and the flesh has a reddish tinge. With warmth and high humidity, the fruits will be larger and of better quality, the colour will also be good. The fruit is virtually seedless, is sweet and juicy and has become extremely popular with consumers. The fruit matures in November.

WHITE MARSH GRAPEFRUIT

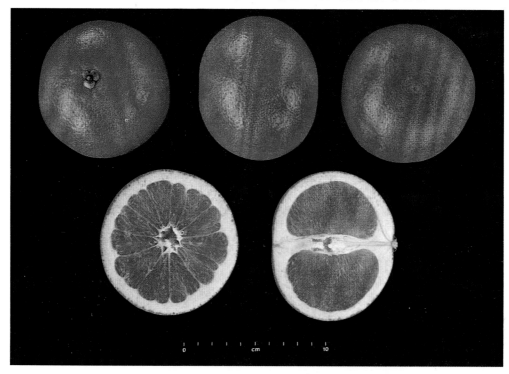

RED BLUSH GRAPEFRUIT

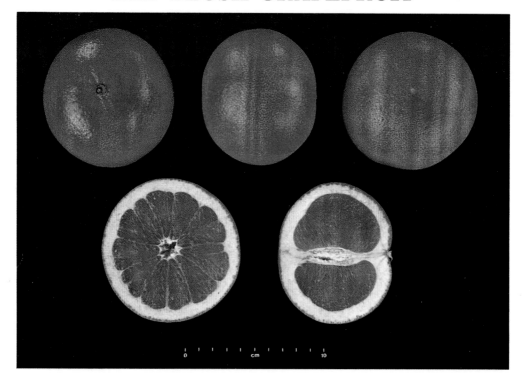

VERNA LEMON

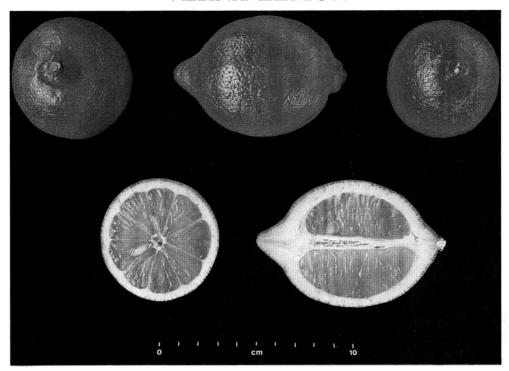

FINO LEMON

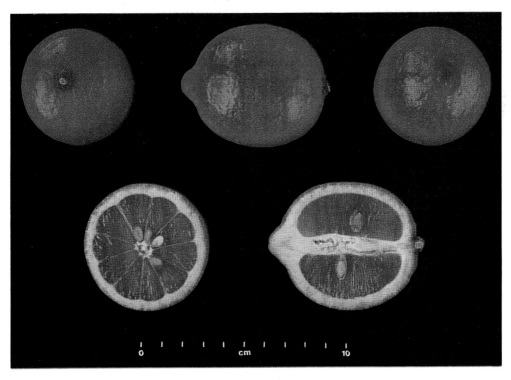

Lemons

VERNA LEMON
citrus limon

The Verna lemon is a Spanish variety and not generally grown elsewhere. The tree is vigorous, with few thorns. The fruits are large with a thick skin and few seeds. They have a high juice content. The fluorescent lemon colour is more pronounced at the ends of the fruits.

This variety may produce up to three crops a year if well fed. The main crop is produced from the Spring flowers and can be collected from February to July the following year. Fruits produced from the summer flowers can be collected from August the following year. These later crops known as the Verdi crops, have a thinner skin and the shape is more round. Both types of fruit will stay on the tree for a long time in good condition. There will be lemons in all stages of development on the tree at the same time.

In Spain, lemon is the only variety that is still allowed to be grafted on to the sour orange root-stock. This is because of the difficulty in grafting lemons on to other root-stock. They will not graft onto Carrizo which is one of the newly developed root-stocks now used in Spain, but will graft onto Troyer.

FINO LEMON

Also known as Mesero, Blanco and Primofiori. This variety is vigorous but does produce thorns. It is a Spanish variety of unknown origin although thought to have been produced from a seed of the Common Lemon. It is very productive with a larger main crop than the Verna.

The fruit is slightly inferior to the Verna, smaller with less juice, but the juice is of high quality and high acidity. The shape is more round and the skin is quite thin. There is a medium quantity of seeds.

If well fed, this variety may produce more than one crop, but the second crop will not be of the quantity of the main crop.

EUREKA LEMON

This variety was originally obtained from California in 1858 and is thought to be a descendant of the lemon Lunario. It is widely grown in many countries of the world and is gaining popularity now in Spain.

The tree is vigorous with few thorns. The fruits are a good size and they have a large quantity of juice which is of excellent quality, with few seeds.

This tree is highly productive. The main crop extends from October to February but will set more fruit during the year particularly if it is well fed. In the early years this tree produces better than the Fino and the Lisbon, but later the heavy crops of both of these will exceed the Eureka.

The spreading habit of the Eureka will enable this tree to be shaped for container growing, but it has a more open habit and is not as densely foliated as others. The fruits are not as hidden as most other citrus which tend to hide their fruits in the centre of the canopy.

LISBON LEMON

The name of this variety is a sure indication that it originated in Portugal, although it is thought that it arrived there as a seed from the Gallego Lemon from Northern Spain, which may account for the fact that it is more cold-hardy than other varieties.

The tree is vigorous and grows to a large size with dense foliage but it is very thorny. It is very productive with good size fruits containing juice of good quality and acidity. There are a few seeds.

The tree holds much of it's fruit in the centre to protect it from adverse conditions and if the tree is well fed it may produce more than one crop.

111

EUREKA LEMON

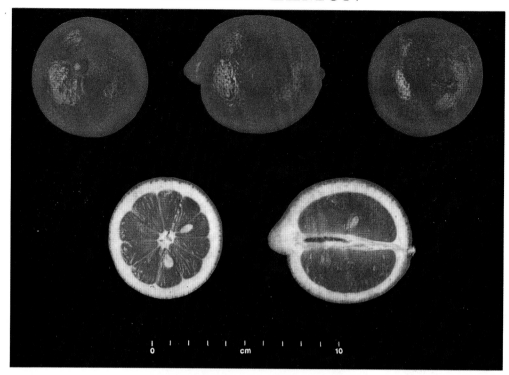

LISBON LEMON

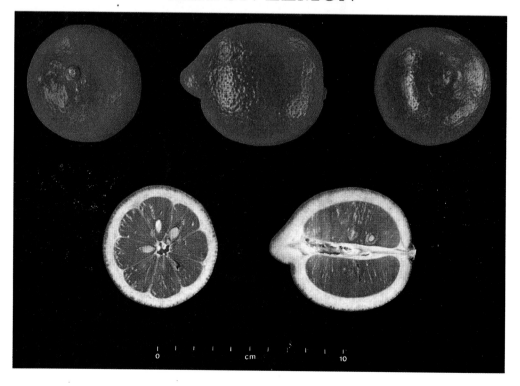

Kumquat Tree
part of the Citrus Collection at the Brogdale Trust

MEYER LEMON

This variety is extremely popular with the keen gardener because it is small, bushy and slow growing. The reason for this is it's exceptional ability to grow from cuttings, but without root-stock it lacks vigour. Unfortunately this also means that it is often susceptible to root-rot and great care should be taken to make sure there is sufficient grit mixed with the compost to provide good drainage and help prevent this.

Meyer Lemon is in fact not a true lemon and is thought to have been crossed with a mandarin. The fruit lacks the acidity of the lemons, being of sweet flavour. It has a smooth rounded shape, is thin skinned with many seeds. Some people find they can eat this lemon straight from the tree because of the sweetness. Meyer Lemon is readily available in most garden centres in the UK and has therefore become a prized possession in many British households although many owners experience difficulties with it. The main cause of this is incorrect feeding.

If well fed, this variety will be constantly flowering and fruiting and is sometimes called 'Four Seasons' although this name is also given to other varieties which have similar fruiting characteristics. Although it is considered to be cold-hardy, it will shed it's leaves in adverse conditions in the same manner as other lemon trees.

Meyer Lemon has been grown extensively in America, and New Zealand as a back-yard plant and at one time was known to be carrying a virus disease. It's availability was restricted although many nurserymen in Britain continued to raise cuttings. There is now a virus free Meyer Lemon called 'Improved Meyer'. Meyer lemon is not produced in Spain as it is not considered to be a commercial variety. We sometimes obtain supplies of this variety from other sources, but we cannot always guarantee to have it on our availability list as we specialise in Spanish Commercial Varieties.

KUMQUAT
Fortunella

Kumquats are related to citrus but have their own genus. The tree shape is small and bushy, with few thorns and has dark green pointed leaves. It produces small oval fruits containing 2-5 seeds in each fruit. The juice although acid, combined with the sweeter rind gives a very pleasant flavour. Kumquats are generally eaten whole, sliced in salads or pickled in brandy.

Growing Instructions

CHOOSING YOUR POT

Growing citrus successfully in the UK generally means using a container. The choice of container is down to personal preference and availability, but there are some aspects that should be taken into account. Citrus trees should be kept moist at all times and not be allowed to dry out, but good drainage is also very important.

The shape of the pot needs careful choice. Do not choose a pot with a wide body and narrow neck as it will be very difficult to take out the root-ball when you need to repot. The base should be fairly broad to give stability to the pot and stop it blowing over in the wind. The depth is perhaps more important than the width as the root system will be deeper than it is wide.

Citrus trees do not require large pots in proportion to their size. The root-stock remains quite compact and over-potting is not necessary and may cause difficulties when moving the tree. An indication that the tree requires re-potting is when the tree appears to be lifting out of the pot, with many of the roots appearing on top of the compost. The roots are trying to grow deeper, but only succeed in pushing the tree up in the pot. The feeding roots are on the surface and should not be unduly disturbed. A top-up of ericaceous compost may be all that is necessary.

Concrete containers, because of the lime content in the cement should not be used for ericaceous (lime hating) plants, such as rhododendrons and camellias, and especially not for citrus. They are also very heavy. Add to that the weight of your citrus tree and you will have great difficulty in moving them.

The solution to this problem is to double pot. Planting your tree in a lightweight plastic container and then putting that into the concrete container for decoration or effect. This would have an added advantage of insulating the roots from the hot sun. Peat or stones can be placed between the two pots which should then be kept moist.

Stoneware pots are made from ball clay which is white. It is then fired at very high temperatures, vitrifying the clay, making it dense like stone. These pots are often varnished and decorated with oriental patterns. Water will not pass through the wall of these pots, so like plastic pots, they must have good drainage. They are usually quite heavy.

TERRA PERMA

LOOK LIKE TERRACOTTA

but with added advantages

LIGHTWEIGHT

UNBREAKABLE

FROST-PROOF

RETAIN MOISTURE

KEEP CLEAN

Terra Perma pots are now available which look exactly like terracotta, even the texture is similar and when potted up you have to touch them to be sure. These are made from ultra modern U.V. protected polymers so they won't fade or crack. They are much lighter in weight than terracotta which means they are easier to move. It may also mean that they will have a tendency to blow over when planted with tall trees, so it would be important when planting to incorporate a good mix of horticultural grit with the compost to add some weight to the pot.

Because the pot is not porous, water and salts do not pass through the wall of the pot, so the pot remains clean. The compost retains more moisture but there is a danger of over watering if grit is not mixed with the compost, or if there are insufficient drainage holes in the base of the pot. These pots are usually purchased without holes in them, and therefore you must make sure you drill sufficient holes to allow for good drainage.

Wooden containers such as half barrels and versailles tubs can also be used, but as the tree will require moving into the conservatory in the winter, satisfy yourself that they can be placed on a tray to collect any drainage from the tub. If using a half barrel, it can be raised using a couple of pieces of wood, or bricks, with a small tray then placed loosely under the base, between these supports. The wood will eventually rot unless it is made of hardwood, but lining the side of the tub with a piece of plastic may give some protection, or double pot as with the concrete container, placing a tray inside under the planted pot to catch the drainage.

Clay or terracotta pots are traditionally the most popular choice. It is said that they allow the plant roots to 'breathe' due to the passage of gasses and liquids through the walls of the pots. The affect of this is that the pots do tend to dry out very quickly and the salts build up on the outside of the pot allowing for the growing of moss and algae. Some people find this very attractive giving a very weathered appearance to the pot, others find it annoying and a lot of hard work trying to keep the pot clean.

The reddish-orange colours vary with the type of clay used and the iron content within the clay. The more iron, the darker the colour. The method of firing also has an effect.

Many pots these days are made simply and cheaply by machine. The big wholesalers deal in such vast quantities that this is so often the only means of manufacture available to them. Pots are made in seconds. Output, quality, shape and delivery times are consistent and uniform. The pots are moulded, ram pressed into the moulds or poured in as clay slip. The clay for mass production of plant pots is very refined and consequently lacks the proper matrix or 'grog' content for porosity and frost resistance.

When the clay is rammed into presses sometimes latent faults, creases and air pockets occur, unpeeling themselves in the frost later, causing flaking. It is likely that the water absorbed by the machine made pot simply freezes it's way out, taking part of the pot with it. Vast quantities of imported machine made pots have quietly crumbled over the length of the British winter. Some even come to grief in their first October.

Mass production sites are found largely in Portugal, Spain, Italy and France but hand thrown pots are still available from these regions. Richard Stevens of Pot Potential, Steventon, Oxfordshire imports Spanish and Portuguese hand thrown pots, but he chooses them with great care checking for quality and durability, before bringing them to the UK. He has a preference for artistic and classical shapes which owe their existence to the functional and practical uses of bygone days.

There is no magic treatment *after* firing that makes pots frost-proof. Attempts at sealing the terracotta (making it impermeable to water) are not 100% and may wear off. This can more often than not impair it's frost resistance by making it more difficult for the water to get out once it has seeped in, and therefore causing a condition of flaking.

Pots placed in sunny locations throughout the winter are more prone to flaking as it is the continuous process of freezing and thawing that is so bad for the pot. It would be preferable if the pot was to remain frozen throughout the whole winter, by keeping it in a shaded or protected part of the garden, where fluctuations of temperature are less noticeable. Thick heavy pots are no better in the frost, in fact the opposite is often true, because the greater differential of temperature between the outside and inside wall surfaces, causes stresses. When using a terracotta pot for citrus trees of course this problem does not arise as the trees are brought in for the winter.

Hand thrown pots, provided they are fired to a high enough temperature are considerably better in the frost than their machine made or moulded counterparts. This could be put down to the fact that

*Pot Potential's Selection of Spanish and Portuguese Pots
as seen at Hampton Court Flower Show 1993 / Richard Stevens*

Hare Lane Pottery, Cranborne, Dorset / Jonathan Garratt

the hand thrown clay is worked more, therefore extracting air pockets which would otherwise become water pockets.

There are still a small number of British Potters who specialize in making hand thrown terracotta pots. Those that fire their kilns with gas, oil or electricity produce pots similar in colour to the continental pots, but Jonathan Garratt of Hare Lane Pottery, near Cranborne in Dorset, fires his kiln with wood. Large wood fired kilns are quite adequate to provide the firing temperatures required and often give the pot some unusual, very desirable colour characteristics with sweeping flame shaped curves of black, red and gold, standing out in contrast and enhancing the curves of the pots themselves. This is produced by the action of the flames from the burning wood.

No firing is the same as another so the results are somewhat unpredictable. For most people this is something of an asset as pots with subtle mellow tones tend to fit comfortably into planting schemes and can be chosen to complement the colours of their contents. Darker pots look good against a red brick background. Each pot has it's place. Although brand new, these pots have an aged look about them and lend a kind of instant maturity to a garden. In time they become weathered, giving an organic look to the pot.

British potters usually produce pots that are particularly strong because they include a good grade of sand in the clay. This produces a more porous frost resistant pot. Jonathan actually guarantees his pots against frost damage which is rare for a producer of garden-ware. When choosing a pot, look for ones that are gritty and sandy to the touch. Smooth pots often have a disappointingly short life.

The clay he uses is dug from a local pig farm and turned into a slurry by mixing with water in a large tank called a 'blunger'. It is run out through a sieve which holds back the stones, roots and any other organic matter. The clay mix is then left to dry in a 'sun-pan' outdoors until it reaches a pliable consistency, after which it is taken to the 'pugmill', a machine which mixes hard and soft clays into a homogeneous mix for throwing.

Most of the pots are thrown in batches and after a considerable amount of time nursing the pots through the drying stages, pots are stacked in the big round kiln. Stacking can take up to two days to complete. Firing the kiln takes place every six weeks or so. The preferred timber is from local conifer plantations, a source that is renewable. The timber is cut and prepared and loaded by Jonathan and it takes 2 tons of timber for each firing. About 15 hours burning time is needed for the kiln to reach the required temperature of 1060°C after which the kiln is left to cool for three days before the 'wicket' or door is unbricked.

Emptying or 'drawing' the kiln takes another two days. Inevitably some pots emerge with small cracks as a result of the firing, but even these are remarkably strong and usually last for years in spite of their defects. They are sold as seconds.

Most of Jonathan's designs derive from European, West African and Chinese pots, with decoration being left fairly quiet, so as not to detract from the plants. Some geometric patterns left on the pots by the use of various roulettes, complement the fluid, natural lines of the plants. This is the combination that Jonathan looks for.

Some pots are left undecorated, with just the colours and shape for interest. Typical of these are the 'Long Toms' a form developed by the Victorians for tomatoes and deep rooting plants. Essentially they are tall, straight sided pots, tapering toward the base. Made in a variety of sizes, they are remarkably versatile and are particularly useful for window-sills, where cuttings and small plants can be observed easily without being left to get cold or dry.

COMPOST

Citrus trees need a slightly acid environment. The pH should be between 6 and 6.5, (lemons slightly lower pH than oranges) so use ericaceous compost. Do not use composts containing lime as they will have a higher pH. Most multi-purpose composts also contain lime and have a fairly high pH so should be avoided. Keep the compost open by using an additive mixture such as horticultural grit, sand and grit mixture, or coarse grit. This will improve the drainage and prevent over watering. Don't be tempted to use left over builders sand as this may contain lime.

A citrus tree planted in a compost with a pH of 7 or over instead of the 6 to 6.5 will mean the tree cannot absorb half the iron you may be giving it, or two thirds of the magnesium. In other words, it seriously affects the trace element absorption. The tree will appear sluggish, under-developed, have dull looking leaves which become very yellow, and will often have little or no sign of new growth. The fruit will be small and underdeveloped and generally the tree will look quite sad.

122

We have found that although it is stated in the Spanish farmers manual that citrus prefer 6 - 6.5, they actually do better at 6.5 - 7. Also the ericaceous compost referred to in this book was, at the time of writing, thought to provide the correct level of acidity, this has since proved to be incorrect and it is in fact nearer to 4.5. Please be advised that multipurpose compost has a pH of 5.5 and is also too acid. John Innes No.3 (for trees and shrubs) being a soil based compost does have a pH of about 6.5 and seems to be more pH stable than peat based composts and needs little or no adjustment. It is advisable though to add some bark chippings to aid the drainage as it may be a little too heavy and slow draining causing problems in the winter. A specialist citrus compost is now available from most garden centres. However, if you prefer to mix your own compost, then we have found the following mix to be satisfactory:- 35% Coir, (made from coconut fibre which has a pH of 6.5 that will not change), 35% sterilised soil (only use if pH is between 6.5 and 7), 20% bark chippings (small enough for use in a potting mix), and 10% grit. This mix is available direct from Global Orange Groves for local customers, but it is too heavy to send mail order.

FEEDING

Citrus trees require an intensive feeding programme continued throughout the year. They need a high nitrogen formula for the summer to boost bushiness and growth and to help prevent fruit drop and premature ripening of immature fruits.

Citrus trees must be fed in the winter. They should still be actively growing, ripening or developing fruit before and after Christmas. Before Easter they may well be covered in blossom. If they are not fed, they will struggle, will produce little or no blossom, but if they do, the tree will not be strong enough to hold the fruit.

The main problem of fruit drop is caused by lack of winter food. The winter feed should be a balanced formula and should contain all the seven trace elements that are essential for a strong and healthy tree. They especially require iron, magnesium, manganese and zinc. The quality of the fruit itself is controlled by the trace elements. It is disappointing to have grown a good sized fruit only to open it and find it is all pith, or extremely poor quality.

We have our own fertilizers prepared especially for citrus trees, and they should be used at the ratio of quarter of a teaspoon to one pint of water or one teaspoon to four pints. The amount given to each tree will depend on it's size, age and pot size. Give sufficient of the mixture to thoroughly soak the compost once a week. The fertilizer can be mixed in a holding tank or used in a diluter.

Compare the chart of analysis of your usual fertilizer against the requirements of citrus trees and you will see why it is essential to use the correct food. The analysis was taken from the product label and was correct at the time of going to press.

Our **'Summer Food for Citrus Trees'** contains;- Nitrogen (N), Phosphates (P) and Potash (K) in the ratio of 25-15-15, plus high levels of 7 essential trace elements. Our **'Winter Food for Citrus Trees'** contains;- N.P.K. 20-20-20, and also contains the same high levels of 7 essential trace elements.

Nitrogen.
Nitrogen is the growth maker, encouraging your tree to develop it's full potential. It is also essential to fruit setting, and lack of nitrogen during the flowering and fruit-setting stage will affect the amount of fruit the tree will produce. Many people use a high potash food at this time and wonder why they have fruit drop.

Lack of nitrogen will also be a contributory factor to excessive or premature leaf loss. Citrus trees are deciduous and will lose their leaves during late winter and early spring, but normally they should not do so until the new leaves have started to appear. Too much nitrogen in the winter months will mean the tree is more sensitive to cold weather, producing weak and tender growth that is easily damaged.

The symptom of nitrogen deficiency is yellowing of the older lower leaves. The summer formula for citrus trees has the higher nitrogen content and should be used from the end of March. A good time to change over is when the clocks change for 'British Summer Time'. This summer formula will stimulate new growth and blossom, and help to slow down excessive leaf loss at this time and will develop the fruit to it's full size.

Phosphorous.
Phosphates are root-makers, and are therefore essential to good root growth. If your tree is lacking phosphorous the growth will be restricted, there will be less blossom and the fruit may be mis-shapen, coarse and thick skinned. An excess of phosphorus in the compost may prevent the absorption of other nutrients.

124

All fertilizers are produced for a specific purpose, the details of the recommended use should be on the label.
We are only advising readers that the following fertilizers, not having been produced for citrus trees,
do not contain their requirements. It does not infer they are unsuitable for the purpose for which they were intended.
The following chart of analysis was taken from the product labels. The details were correct at the time of going to press.

ANALYSIS OF FERTILIZERS

	N	P	K	
Summer Food for Citrus	25	15	15	7 Essential Trace Elements at High Strength
Winter Food for Citrus	20	20	20	7 Essential Trace Elements at High Strength

PRODUCT	N	P	K	TRACE ELEMENTS
Maxicrop	5	5	5	6 Trace Elements at low strength. No Magnesium
Tomorite	4	4.5	8	No Trace Elements
Unifeed	14	14	14	No Trace Elements
Miracle-Gro	15	30	15	6 Trace Elements. No Magnesium
Vitax Q4	5.3	7.5	10	6 Trace Elements. No Zinc
Liquinure	8	4	4	Small amounts of 3 Trace Elements. No Zinc
Phostrogen	10	10	27	Small amounts of 3 Trace Elements. No Zinc
Evergrow	20	20	20	No Trace Elements
Baby-Bio	10.6	4.4	1.7	No Trace Elements
Keri-Grow	6	4	4	No Trace Elements
Deep Feed	7	3	4	6 Trace Elements. No Zinc
Gromore	7	7	7	No Trace Elements
Ericaceous	5	4	7	5 Trace Elements. No Magnesium and No Zinc
Miracid	30	10	10	6 Trace Elements. No Magnesium (May cause over-acidity)
Fish Blood & Bone	6	5	4	No Trace Elements
Chempak 2	25	15	15	7 Trace Elements at one fifth strength
Chempak 3	20	20	20	7 Trace Elements at one fifth strength

Potassium.

Potash is considered to be a ripening agent and it enhances the fruit quality, but given in excess the fruits are coarser with a higher acid content and delayed maturity. Too little and the fruit will have a thin skin, may split easily and will not hold on the tree. The 'Winter Food for Citrus Trees' has a balanced formula with a higher potash content and less nitrogen than the summer formula and should be used from the end of October until the end of March. Most citrus fruits ripen between October and March, this is why the tree should still be fed at this time. It is the lowering of temperatures that ripens the fruit not the hot sun.

Magnesium.

Magnesium is important in the development of the fruit colour. Lack of magnesium will cause the tree to have poor growth and increased sensitivity to cold. This will become apparent in the autumn particularly in container grown trees. It is advisable to foliar feed the trees regularly with our citrus fertilizers which will help to correct this. If the trees are given manure as a fertilizer they often lack magnesium.

Manganese.

A deficiency in manganese will cause reduced growth and less fruit, it shows first in the newest growth with 'shading' appearing in the leaves, and general lack of lustre and rich colour.

Zinc.

A deficiency of zinc will also reduce growth and harvest, and is shown as interveinal chlorosis or 'yellowing'. The best way to describe it is like yellow highlights contrasting sharply with the deeper green of the veins. This effect becoming more obvious in varying stages of deficiency, again showing in the newest growth first. The leaves may become almost spotted with green, the main area of the leaf having become very pale or yellow.

Copper.

Fruit quality, as well as fruit production is affected by copper deficiency. It is shown in the fruit as 'pockets' around the pith. Copper deficiency can be quite common in trees grown in peat composts, but our fertilizers contain sufficient copper to correct this.

Iron.

Too much lime in the compost is the main cause of iron deficiency as well as the constant use of tap-water known to contain lime.

$\mathfrak{C}$ITRUS $\mathfrak{C}$ARE $\mathfrak{K}$IT

EVERYTHING YOU NEED FOR YOUR CITRUS TREES

INCLUDES:-

250g 'SUMMER FOOD FOR CITRUS TREES'

Aims to boost bushiness and growth.
Helps prevent fruit drop and premature ripening of immature fruits.
Helps develop fruit to it's full size.

250g 'WINTER FOOD FOR CITRUS TREES'

A balanced formula for natural sustained winter activity.
including fruit ripening.
Helps prevent premature leaf fall.
Prepares tree for Spring Blossom.

100g FLOWERS OF SULPHUR

Reduces pH in hard water areas for better
trace element absorption and improved leaf colour.

OUR PRODUCTS AND GROWING INSTRUCTIONS ARE PROMOTED BY TELEVISION GARDENING PRESENTERS AND GARDENING CORRESPONDENTS

BECAUSE THEY REALLY WORK!

THEY ARE NOW USED BY THE HEAD GARDENERS OF STATELY HOMES AND PALACES AND BY THOUSANDS OF SATISFIED CUSTOMERS

(available in some Garden Centres and by Mail Order)
send S.A.E. for details

Global Orange Groves UK Citrus Care Kit

The increased pH or alkalinity, prevents the roots absorbing iron and it is shown as a noticeable veining on the leaves and a gradual all over paling of the leaves to almost no colour at all in severe cases. Symptoms show first in the new growth.

Boron.
A deficiency in boron can be identified as the leaves become thick, curled, wilted and yellow. The branches produce small twiggy growths. Too much boron will produce browning of the leaf margins. This is not to be confused with the browning caused by excessive heat when the trees are kept next to the glass in a conservatory or green house. This will show as a crisp dry browning where the leaf has been literally burnt.

Molybdenum.
Molybdenum is essential to all plants and a deficiency causes a condition known as yellow spotting.

Calcium.
Calcium is essential to all plants but has not been included in our fertilizers as it is thought to be in sufficient concentration naturally in the water. Lack of calcium however will result in stunting of the growth tips, shedding of blossom, weakening of the stems and possible death of the tree. If you use only rainwater on your trees and after eliminating all other possibilities feel your tree is in need of calcium, it can be given as calcium nitrate which is found in gypsum. This would also give the tree sulphur. Using water from a water softener may give rise to calcium deficiency as virtually all trace minerals are removed from the water. Don't worry about it, but just be aware that an occasional dose may be required.

TEMPERATURE

Citrus trees are essentially out door plants and prefer cool, not hot conditions and plenty of fresh air. This surprises most people as it is thought that they need hot Mediterranean climates in order to flourish. The trees protect themsleves by generally producing a dense canopy of leaves under which is hidden the fruit, away from the damage caused by the sun or indeed any excessively cold temperatures or frost. The trunk is either short, shaded by the canopy, or is not exposed at all, being completely covered by the foliage as a protection. In California they actually paint the trunks of citrus trees with a latex mixture to protect the exposed trunk from the sun which could otherwize be damaged by sun-burn.

Most citrus trees enjoy the early morning dew, although there are a few which do not. These particular trees, should be avoided in the British climate for obvious reasons. The trees should be kept outside as much as possible only being brought in just prior to frost.

When inside under glass, a minimum temperature of about 50°-55°F (10°-12°C) would be ideal in order to maintain growing conditions. Temperatures lower than this may cause the tree to go dormant at a time when you are expecting the fruit to come to full ripening condition. Lemons in particular should have a good crop of young developing fruit at this time and will need to be active. Frost will damage tender winter growth and blossom, severe frost will damage winter fruit, and may kill the tree. The tree is more likely to withstand a frost in the autumn than in the spring as the leaves will have hardened during the summer, but in the early spring there will be many new and tender shoots.

Sudden and extreme changes of temperature may result in loss of leaves, but this is not necessarily fatal to the tree. Very low temperatures may cause the leaves to curl under, this is not detrimental to the tree but will be a little unsightly. It does not reverse once it has happened, but these leaves will be shed when the new leaves appear.

If the tree does not take up water it is an indication that the temperature is too low, possibly at night, which is the most vulnerable time. This would mean the tree is not absorbing food and the next problem you will encounter is dormancy and leaf fall.

You may prefer to protect your tree from extreme cold by covering it with a suitable material such as polythene, bubble insulation film, or a light material or webbing especially made for the purpose, but it is always best to protect the growing shoots on the tree by using canes to support the material and to prevent it touching the delicate new shoots and blossom.

If it is difficult to raise the temperature, then keep the compost on the dry side, but be aware that leaf loss may occur. The tree will sprout new shoots again when the temperature improves.

VENTILATION

Having several trees in full blossom in confined conditions such as the conservatory or greenhouse can be almost overpowering. It is necessary for the plants and for yourselves to ventilate well at least once a day, bearing in mind that at this time it could still be frosty and may not be advisable to leave windows open at night.

HUMIDITY

Citrus trees like to have water on their leaves, this keeps them cool, keeps them clean and helps keep them free from pest attack. Spraying or misting the trees during the summer when outside (you can use the garden hose) is essential and during the winter if your conservatory is hot and dry they should also be sprayed.

If it is inconvenient to spray when the tree is inside, you may have to think about taking the tree outside once a week and give it a good hose down or perhaps consider the added benefits of an indoor waterfall.

It is not advisable to keep your citrus trees in the house especially if it is centrally heated. At temperature levels of 68°-70°F (20°C) the trees would require about 50% humidity but the house would only have about 5%-20%. The tree would suffer and leaf loss would occur. You may lose your tree. Improving the humidity can make a dramatic difference to the good health of your tree in these circumstances.

In **cold conditions** however, the reverse is true. Excessive humidity will cause grey mould or *Botrytis* to develop on the blossoms. Raising the temperature may help to prevent this, but sometimes causes more humidity. It may be necessary to insulate the glass house or conservatory to prevent excessive humidity or isolate the tree by building a protective frame of bamboo canes covered with polythene. Experiment and see which is best for your situation. Keeping the tree on the drier side in winter may help and the use of a suitable chemical spray may help to prevent *Botrytis* developing.

INDOOR WATERFALLS

Some people prefer to keep their citrus trees in the conservatory, orangery or greenhouse all the year round. One way of overcoming the problems of overheating and lack of humidity is by the use of indoor waterfalls. These can be made to measure, any size or dimension, to suit your particular environment. The benefits of 'moving water' in the atmosphere is quite dramatic both to the plants and to people themselves.

Tony Benham, from Canterbury in Kent, had lived most of his life near water, owned a watermill at one time and restored it, but it was not until he was looking into rock pools while on holiday in Cornwall that he was inspired to combine water with his potting skills and decided to make waterfalls.

Tony incorporates planting pockets and pots for ferns and trailing plants in his waterfall designs and he has found that the plants seem to be happier in irregular forms rather than the usual round pots made on the potter's wheel. In irregular shaped planting pockets, the plants seem to nestle better, more in keeping with their natural environment. Other plants in the room also benefit thriving in the cooler, cleaner, more humid atmosphere, and people notice the difference too, particularly in the conservatory.

While the waterfall is a piece of ceramic sculpture it has to be functional as well. With water and electricity working together, safety has to be paramount and so safety features are built in.

The waterfalls are completely self contained, having their own pump and filter system, they constantly recycle the same water and do not need to be connected to a water supply. Evaporation of the water will take place, so a top up will be required for the waterfall from time to time. Always use filtered water or strained rain water, as using tap water containing too much lime, particularly if you are in a hard water area, will mean you get a build up of lime deposits and algae.

Waterfalls provide a combination of visual impact and sound. Molten glass is used in areas where the water flows so a small spot light on the waterfall really brings it alive. The waterfalls can be used outside on the patio and need not be confined to the conservatory or the house.

Ceramic Waterfalls/Tony Benham

They are best displayed on natural materials such as wood, but can also be placed on brickwork, as part of an architectural feature such as an old fireplace, a recess or stone shelf, just on piles of bricks or on logs. To look their best they have to blend in and as the plants develop around them, so of course they become more a part of the space and environment. Lighting can be used to great effect.

In the manufacture of the waterfalls, Tony finds the combined use of water and clay a stimulating, exciting and thrilling experience. The results are unpredictable and often the water seems to go up hill and not where directed. If it works well and makes a sound recognisable from nature, it is very satisfying. In the early days the water sounded more like a running tap than a babbling brook, but getting the water to run in an irregular way across broken surfaces and forming little patterns is a really big part of the quality that Tony is now after. The *sound* has to be right.

The sound of water is associated with relaxation and healing and many people working in areas of therapy are now installing waterfalls in their clinics for the beneficial and therapeutic effects they produce.

With any of the designs you can add your own sea shells, pebbles, and plants and they can be moved around to change the flow or the sound of the water. Waterfalls can be made to suit particular spaces of the house, they can be a metre across or a third of that size, they can be made to fit in the corner of a room where it will nestle in and enhance or complete a design. Perhaps you prefer a wall panel waterfall, rather like a rock face, where the water trickles down into a small recess. There is an incredible quality of peace and calm about the Bhudda waterfall especially when lit with a candle.

Recently a waterfall was purchased by an elderly lady who had been left a bag of stones collected by her father from a beach where he had been wounded during the first world war. She had kept these stones and could not bring herself to throw them away, but could find no use for them. The waterfall was an excellent way of displaying and using them.

Another lady bought a waterfall because it recreated the sound of a stream she was familiar with in her childhood.

A music room sounds an unlikely place for a waterfall, but one of Tony's customers bought a waterfall for that purpose. She found that the waterfall cleansed the atmosphere resulting in a sharper and clearer musical tone which was very much appreciated.

The process of making, begins with the mixing of the clay. Tony mixes his own clays from powder blended from sand and fire clay from Derbyshire, but adds other ingredients including rust particles saved from the restoration of his old watermill. After mixing the clay it is put through a machine called a 'pugmill' which extrudes the clay, putting it under pressure and squeezing out the air bubbles. It is then covered and stored, until required.

A measured weight is taken, according to the size of slab required for the design. This is rolled with a rolling pin at which point additional colours are added. The clay is then placed on a shallow mould which shapes the base of the waterfall. Other pieces are built on top of this to form the contours and design required. The model is then left to harden off until it gets to what is known as a 'green state' or 'cheese hard state' at which point additional pots can be added for the plants. The complete unit is then put out in the sun to dry, but is not allowed to dry too quickly, as it may dry unevenly.

The firing of the kiln helps with the drying process, particularly in the winter as it is an indoor kiln and heats the whole studio. The kiln is fired every two to three weeks. When the waterfalls are really dry they are glazed using a unique blend of ashes collected from the hop fields in Kent, mixed with local clays and additional oxides, giving a good celadon green glaze. Applied by brush, blended and smoothed by hand, producing a finish, varied in colour and texture, enhancing the form and contours of the waterfall.

The firing of the kiln does affect the colours immensely and in order to get the very important speckled variegated texture, it is necessary to fire the waterfalls in a kiln where the 'breathing' (mix of oxygen and gas) of the kiln can be controlled. A gas kiln is preferred for this purpose and is fired to 1265°C. A slow firing time is required because of the thickness of the pieces so it takes about 24 hours for the kiln to get hot.

At one point in the firing, the airflow has to be changed in order to control the atmosphere in the kiln. This change enables the oxides in the metals to revert to their original metal form, and the process is known as 'reduction'. This causes the speckles and richer colours in the clay and is due to the iron particles (rust) which are present not only in the uncoloured clay, but to appear through and in the glaze as well. The reduction of oxygen will affect all the colours in the kiln.

It is difficult in a large kiln to get the kiln to breathe evenly and to get consistent colour changes. Sometimes they are great, sometimes they do not come out quite as expected, but this is part of the excitement.

Once the kiln has finished, it is sealed and left to cool, a stage which takes a further 24 hours. There is a wonderful feeling in the workshop of peace and achievement when the kiln has finished firing.

WATERING

Citrus trees should be kept moist at all times and not allowed to dry out when kept in containers. The type of container used will have some effect on the tree's requirements, but also the weather and the speed of growth of the tree. If the weather is hot, the tree may require water every day.

The temperature plays an important part in water take up in winter, because if the temperature goes too low, the tree stops taking up water and goes dormant. If this happens, the compost may remain soggy, root rot may set in and the tree suffer. Raising the temperature is the ideal solution. If you had correctly planted your tree with sufficient grit in the compost, it should drain well enough if the water is not used by the tree, but if you know temperature is going to be a problem, keep the tree on the drier side in winter.

Long periods of continuous rain when the tree is standing outside will have the effect of washing out the fertilizer, which will cause a weakening of the tree, so cover the pot with a polythene apron to prevent over watering and make sure you continue to feed the tree as required.

Peat based compost contain magnesium carbonate or lime which is used to build up the pH to an acceptable level. This gets washed out by continuous watering and may need replacing. Adjusting the pH of the water is a way of restoring the pH of the compost and makes sure the adjustment reaches through to the roots.

During the winter it is advisable not to use freezing cold water from an outside tap to water your trees. This will affect your trees, cause the

136

leaves to curl under and will also prevent water absoption through the roots. You are trying to keep the temperature at 50°-55°F (10°-12°C) so giving your tree water that may be just above freezing rather defeats the object.

Water that has been through a water softener has had practically all it's natural trace elements and chemicals taken out. This is perfectly alright to use on your citrus trees, but there is a possibility that your tree will be short of calcium. The additional salt content caused by this process should not have any harmful effect on your tree. If you use softened water on other houseplants it is essential to feed them.

PRUNING

Citrus trees can be pruned to the desired shape and size at any time, however it would be better to prune your tree immediately after fruiting and before the new growth starts to appear. This would then encourage the tree to produce new branches within the area and size you require instead of extending it's width and height. With a continuously fruiting variety this may mean sacrificing any blossom or fruit that may be on the tree at the time. January or February would be the preferred time.

There are no special instructions, but the tree will produce a branch from each leaf node so take this into account when cutting back in order to produce a good shape. Cut back to a leaf node that is pointing in the direction you would like to see the new growth take, i.e. pointing upwards and not down, although it is natural for new growth to seek out the light and to grow up rather than down. You do not need to be too particular.

The fruit is produced on old and new wood and even a quite mature, bare branch or trunk can sprout new growth. Take off any shoots that sprout below the graft as you do not want to encourage the root-stock to take over.

Forming your tree into a standard may mean that you cut away a lot of fruiting branches. As a protection against the hot sun, and any winter frost, the citrus tree produces most of it's fruit in the centre, hidden amongst the leaves and branches, so don't be too hasty removing the centre growth. There are one or two varieties that do produce at the ends of the branches, such as the Eureka.

In the Spring, the citrus tree may produce a very vigorous new shoot that seems to be larger that the others with much bigger leaves. This is quite normal and it is not necessary to remove this shoot or shoots, as the tree will grow to fill any gaps and incorporate this vigorous growth into the overall shape of the tree.

You may feel however that this new growth is out of proportion to the shape you are maintaining for your tree and in which case the shoot can be cut back to a more agreeable size or trained to become a sturdy branch using loose ties to hold it in the exact position you require. These shoots are often called 'watershoots'.

It is always preferable to prune your tree annually, or pinch out the tips of the new growth when it reaches the desired length as this will produce a better shaped tree with regularly shaped branches. If pruning is left too long the branches will have become quite thick and pruning will be more of a task and the results could be rather unsightly. A hard pruning on a mature tree may help to improve it's vigor if the tree is looking tired, but generally improved feeding may be all that is necessary.

ROOT-STOCK

Until about 1840 most citrus trees were produced from seedlings, due partly to the ease with which seeds could be transported world-wide, but root-rot *Phytophthora* became a major disease with this method of propagation and budding trees on to tolerant rootstocks has become the normal method.

Sour orange was used extensively, because of it's ability to produce good yields of high quality fruit, but was found to be susceptible to citrus *Tristeza* virus. In Spain the use of sour orange as a root-stock is prohibited by law, except for lemons, although it is still being used in other countries.

The use of rough lemon as a root-stock produces fruits of poor quality, thicker, coarser rind, a lower juice content and the juice itself is low in sugars. It is less cold-hardy, intolerant to blight and is susceptible to root-rot and to burrowing nematodes. Inspite of this it is used in a number of countries including Florida and Australia.

Trifoliate orange is regarded as being a semi-dwarfing root-stock, producing fruits of outstanding quality. The trifoliate tree is deciduous and can be extremely cold hardy so it is used in relatively cold parts of Japan. It is susceptible to *Exocortis* and blight and to a similar disease *Marchitamiento Repentino*.

There are a number of rootstocks available to-day, but the most widely used are man-made hybrids called 'Troyer' and 'Carrizo'. They resulted from crosses of trifoliate orange and navel orange and are very similar in many respects.

Fruit quality is similar to that of the sour orange. Trees on Troyer and Carrizo are resistant to *Xyloporosis* but susceptible to blight and are less cold hardy than those of other root-stocks. They now account for 70% of new plantings in Spain and they have also become important root-stocks in Florida and are being used increasingly in other parts of the world. Oranges can be grown on both Troyer and Carrizo, but lemons are not compatible with Carrizo so are grown on Troyer and to a limited extent on Sour Orange when necessary.

The choice of root-stock will affect the tree health, the yield, the fruit quality and size as well as other horticultural characteristics. The trees that we supply from Spain are all treated with 'Anti-Virus' against a number of diseases, as plant health is of prime importance.

POLLINATION AND FRUITING

There are so many new varieties of citrus fruits to-day, all of which are hybrids produced either by spontaneous mutations or by special selection. This means that trees grown from pips or seeds taken from fruits purchased in the shops are unlikely to fruit, not being original varieties. All sweet juicy fruits sold to-day are propagated by grafting or budding.

Some lemon and grapefruit pips may produce fruit as they are not quite as hybridized as the oranges, but only if fed correctly, although correct feeding is not a guarantee, as it does depend on the variety chosen. It may take many years for the trees to come into bearing especially as they are being container grown. To guarantee success from a seed, grow a Seville Marmalade Orange, (Naranja Amarga) as this is always propagated in this way and should start to produce blossom after three years.

Citrus trees are self pollinating, in fact majority set fruit without pollination as the flowers do not contain viable pollen. This condition is known as *Parenthocarpy*. Some normally seedless varieties may produce seeds if their flowers have been cross pollinated with another variety. Spain is the only country to produce a truly seedless Clementine and farmers try to avoid cross pollination by growing large groups of one variety together and by having a variety that will not cross pollinate in the next field.

Citrus fruits are generally harvested between October and March, depending on variety. It is the lowering of seasonal temperatures that develops the colour, although the amount of warm sun during the growing season may affect the amount of sugars contained in the fruit. Too much heat during the ripening stage may prevent the colour forming and the fruit may remain green. It can also be said that immature fruits exposed to too much cold will change colour prematurely, but can be re-greened with a raise in temperature. This is why the best oranges are grown in sub-tropical climates and why you only see green oranges in the tropics. Colour is an important marketing feature and can be controlled in artificial conditions prior to shipping.

Blossom is produced during the winter, early spring, and sometimes as late as June, but some citrus trees may produce blossom more than once in the year, some varieties, but not all, appear to be perpetually in flower and fruit, and this gives citrus trees a 'general' reputation for fruiting and blossoming at the same time. It is important when the tree is in flower that it is kept fairly cool, a heat wave or excessive indoor temperature at this time will cause the blossom to fall with the resultant lack of fruit. They should also be well watered and well fed at this time. Nitrogen is important for successful fruit set and our 'Summer Food for Citrus Trees' should be used from the end of March.

It is not necessary to thin the fruitlets. The tree will shed any fruit it cannot hold.

Minneolas and Lemons growing in Yorkshire / F David Heaton

Clementines and Grapefruits growing in Essex
Dennis Sullivan

SUCCESS STORIES

The following are excerpts from letters received from customers who are successfully growing citrus in different parts of the UK.

Mr F David Heaton is growing citrus as far north as Yorkshire. They have been planted directly into the soil within his greenhouse but are given plenty of ventilation in the summer. The photograph shows his Minneola and a lemon tree.

Mr Dennis Sullivan is growing a Clementine and a Grapefruit in his greenhouse in Essex. he writes "....the trees are kept in a humid environment and are about 5 years old. The temperature in the winter can be as low as 30°F (0°C) and rising in the summer to 120°F (50°C) but to compensate for this heat, there is a fish pond in the greenhouse which creates the humidity."

Mrs Smart from Sussex wrote "....My small citrus trees look very well with using your fertilizer. A small 20 year old Calamondin Orange has a mass of flower buds on it after sparse crops of flowers for years. My small Villa Franca lemon has at least doubled it's size and has many sprays of buds and flowers, at least 10-15 flowers per spray. A lovely sight to see."

Jane Lloyd of Buckinghamshire wrote "....Please could I have a pot of Winter Food, it's so wonderful, don't know what I did before!"

Mr John Howe of Essex wrote "....I am pleased to advise you that the combination of your good advice and the use of your special citrus fertilizers has saved my favourite lemon tree."

Mrs N Pateman of Suffolk wrote "....Firstly may I say what a difference your 'Summer Food' has made to my lemon tree Calias 'Letitia'. She is now really full of life, fruit and new shoots. Excellent!"

R Minter of Hampshire wrote "....My Verna Lemon is thriving and about to go out of doors for the summer. The Winter Food has been very successful resulting in very heavy flowering and I think a good fruit set."

J A Lockett of Diss wrote "....I used your Winter Food for Citrus Trees last winter on my Meyer Lemon bush to excellent effect."

142

PROBLEMS AND SOLUTIONS

CITRUS DISEASES

Virus diseases in Citrus trees is a major world wide problem. There has been a lot of devastation to such an important agricultural product. Our Spanish trees have been treated with 'Anti-Virus' to the Spanish Ministry of Agriculture permitted levels, against the known citrus diseases of *Tristeza, Psoriasis and Exocortis*. They are tested before being exported from Spain and are virus free. Should these trees be exposed to virus diseases, they should not manifest in the tree. The protection lasts for the life of the tree, but cuttings taken from this stock will only be protected in the first generation. The second generation will not be protected. Not all citrus producing countries treat their trees with 'Anti-Virus'. Spain is the leader in this field.

We do however sometimes stock trees that do not come from Spain. These will not have been treated with 'Anti-Virus' but should have been produced from virus-free stock issued from a licenced nursery.

At one time Meyer Lemon was known to be carrying a virus disease *Phytophthora* and it's availability was restricted. There is now a virus free Meyer Lemon called 'Improved Meyer'.

New EC regulations stipulate that all Citrus producing nurseries in countries where citrus is grown as a commercial crop, are tested annually for virus diseases in their stock, which has led to a great number of nurseries closing down as far as citrus production is concerned. The good news is that the few that are left still producing citrus trees should have a guarantee of quality. Availabilty of citrus may be affected by the reduced number of suppliers. In addition to this, it is now forbidded to bring citrus trees into the EC from elsewhere.

The movement of citrus within the EC is very much restricted with some countries having a complete ban on the import of citrus trees, and others being more concerned with the export conditions. It is not possible to take trees bought in the UK to your residence in France or Spain, citrus trees would have to be purchased in the country where they will be grown.

It is against regulations to bring citrus trees from Europe to this country without the appropriate paperwork. Citrus is on the list of restricted plants.

PESTS AND THEIR CONTROL

As with other plants, citrus are not immune from pest attack. They can suffer from two-spotted or citrus red spider mites, greenhouse or citrus whitefly, aphids, scale insects, mealybugs, thrips, caterpillars and vine weevils.

Most of these pests are attracted by hot dry conditions especially in enclosed conditions in the winter, and also in early spring when the citrus trees produce their new spring growth. Keep the tree cool and misted to help prevent pest attack. Strong healthy trees are much less likely to be attacked by pest. A weekly inspection taking about two minutes will prevent hours of pest control and could prevent a lot of damage to your tree.

A good wash down with a soapy solution taking care to gently remove all trace of the pests as you spray, should be all that is necessary. A soapy solution should have the effect of blocking the breathing tubes of the pests as well as helping to dislodge them. If you cover the compost before you start, this may help to prevent pests migrating back to the tree for a second attack. With any of these pests, if you have left it too late and feel the need for a chemical pesticide, use *Malathion* which is safe for edible fruit. Double strength will be needed to treat scale insects.

Yellow sticky fly traps which include a pheromone are now available in shops and will help to catch flying pests including moths. The fly-trap can be attached to a cane and inserted in the pot.

There is now another way of dealing with pests for those who are particular about the use of chemicals. Biological pest control is an effective alternative method which has been developed, used and steadily improved over the years by commercial growers. This may be the answer for you.

Chemicals can have toxic effects on humans, pets and the environment, particularly if not used with great care. The smell from chemicals used in enclosed conditions such as a conservatory may be unpleasant and if food is served in the vicinity of the treated trees, or fish kept in an indoor pond, this could be most unwelcome.

With bushy trees, it may be difficult or too time consuming to reach every leaf and stem surface, which would leave untreated patches to re-infect the whole area. Some persistent pests could become immune to the spray you are using and then become almost impossible to eradicate.

Biological pest control is the name given to the use of natural predators and parasitic insects to control specific pests. Before embarking on this course, there are several basic points to be considered.

a) Correct identification of the pest is essential as the beneficial insect is generally specific to a particular pest.

b) You cannot use biological control as a *preventative* measure. These pest controllers require the pests for their own survival and without them they will die.

c) Timing is crucial. The natural predators and parasites should be introduced early in an infestation, not when the pests are really numerous. If an infestation is already out of hand, spray the tree with a soapy solution to reduce the pest problem to a manageable level, removing badly infested leaves and burning them.

d) Chemicals would produce an instant result, but biological control takes time for the pest controllers to establish their natural breeding cycle and gain control. The predators and parasites are very small, generally unnoticeable, which may lead you to believe that they have escaped or died. Patience is paramount. However, if conditions have been favourable, you should start to notice that the infestation is not getting any worse within a month, a definite improvement within 6 weeks and near eradication within 3 months.

e) An ideal situation to aim for is a few pests, sufficient to provide food and breeding places for the pest controllers, but not too numerous to do any damage to your citrus tree. Total eradication is not possible or required with this method.

f) It may be necessary to renew the input of pest controllers at the first signs of any new infestation, as soon as the conditions are suitable.

g) All natural predators and parasites are compatible and can work with each other in the same area.

h) Do not use chemical sprays for at least a month before introducing your natural predators. The exceptions are *Rapid*, for the treatment of greenfly, and soap sprays such as *Savona* and *Safers Concentrated Organic Garden Spray* which can be used around the predators, providing it is not sprayed on them.

i) Temperatures should be above 15°C (60°F) for the insects to work at their best. They will not die until temperatures reduce to near freezing, but they will cease to work, as the rate at which they breed will slow down and they will not keep pace with the pests they are there to control.

j) When your predator population has increased and the biological control is working well, be careful when pruning your citrus trees. Always leave prunings next to the tree in the greenhouse or conservatory for a week or two for the predators and parasites to hatch out and return to the tree.

Red Spider Mites.

There are two types of problem spider mites each having to be treated differently when considering biological control. Both will produce a stickiness or honey-dew on the leaves caused by the mites sucking the sap out of the leaves. The leaf will at first become slightly mottled or speckled with a lack of lustre and may be covered in sooty mould which develops on the stickiness. The leaves will then start to look quite limp, may turn brown and drop off.

The signs to look for are sickly looking top growth, fine webbing and little white specks (moulted skins) and if you look very carefully you may see moving mites on the leaves. They are usually present in hot dry conditions such as those produced in a greenhouse or conservatory and may also be found if the tree is kept in the house over winter. Improving the humidity by spraying the tree should prevent an attack, or at least slow down the rate at which the mites reproduce.

In summer, when temperatures under glass are 20°-30°C (70°-90°F) red spider mites multiply incredibly fast and can cause devastating damage if not controlled early. Spider mites live about 30 days and lay up to 100 eggs a day. A new generation is produced every 8 days.

In cool winters, the mites would crawl off the plants and find warm dry places such as brickwork cavities or under benches to hibernate, but reappear when conditions warm up in the spring. Where a greenhouse or conservatory is kept warm in winter, the spider mites will remain active, but due to the decreased light levels, not as active as in summer.

The Two-Spotted Mite is the most common 'red' spider mite which plagues greenhouse and conservatory owners. It is actually light greenish in colour with two dark spots in summer, but turns red in cooler temperatures during October, losing it's red colour again when the temperature rises in the summer. It prefers to remain on the undersides of leaves and can be effectively treated with a predator mite

Phytoseiulus Persimilis. This is another type of spider mite, which is a shiny orange colour and moves more quickly than it's prey. It eats 5-20 of the sap-sucking mites per day, as well as some of their eggs. In temperatures of 21°C (70°F) it can reproduce twice as fast as it's prey. At temperatures below 15°C (60°F), the rate of reproduction is less than that of their prey. A humid atmosphere is favoured by this mite, so regular misting or damping down of the floor during hot weather helps achieve more rapid control. It is advisable to introduce a second batch of *Phytoseiulus* 2-3 weeks after the first.

Citrus Red Mite is not as commonly encountered as the two spotted mite, it remains red all year round and feeds on both the upper and lower surfaces of the leaves. Good control is not always achieved with *Phytoseiulus Persimilis*, so another predatory mite is used, called *Typhlodromus Occidentalis.* This is more difficult to obtain as the citrus red mite is not a problem commercial growers in the UK have to deal with, so production is very limited.

Whitefly.

As the name suggests, they are little white flies, about 2 mm long which feed on the undersides of leaves from where they suck the sap. They fly up in clouds when disturbed. They lay microscopic eggs, which then hatch out and go through several crawling and static stages until they become clearly visible as creamy-white oval 'scales' on the undersides of leaves. Out of this stage, the adult white fly emerges. They are now highly resistant to chemicals and plague almost every greenhouse and conservatory. In summer the adults live about 20 days and lay about 200 eggs. The time taken from egg to adult is about 26 days.

The first sign of the presence of whitefly is the adults flying around when disturbed. Other signs are a stickiness appearing on leaf surfaces which results from secretion from infestations underneath the leaf above. Any stickiness present on the leaves will quickly develop a sooty mould. Although unsightly, the secretion is not harmful but does impede the work of the beneficial parasite *Encarsia*. The sooty mould can be washed off with soapy water and a sponge. Yellow sticky fly traps can be effectively used to indicate when the first whiteflies are appearing and also to trap adult whiteflies before the introduction of biological controls. There are two types of whitefly.

Greenhouse whitefly *Trialeurodes Vaporariorum* is probably the only one you will have problems with under glass, although citrus is generally not it's favourite host plant.

Encarsia Formosa is a tiny parasitic 'wasp', barely visible to the naked eye, being about 0.6 mm long. They are generally obtained as little black parasitic 'scales' which hatch within 1-7 days of purchase. They lay their eggs in the developing oval whitefly 'scales'. As the eggs develop, they will turn the whitefly 'scale' from white to black, which gives a good indication of their activity.

The time taken from *Encarsia* egg to adult is from 10-31 days, depending on temperature. In high summer their reproduction rate is twice that of the whitefly, but in temperatures below 21°C (70°F) the whiteflies reproduce faster. Female *Encarsia* live 15-31 days and can lay up to 400 eggs. If control seems too slow, a soapy spray can be used at any time after introduction of *Encarsia* to kill the adult whiteflies on the very top growth of the plant, as there will be no *Encarsia* working at the top, only down where the whitefly eggs will be developing.

Citrus whitefly is uncommon in the UK. It looks the same as the Greenhouse whitefly when flying around, but instead of lots of separate oval white scales visible under the leaves, it creates fluffy, sticky, cotton-wool masses under the leaves. This cotton-wool mass differs from Mealybug, because it is not generally in leaf axes or hidden crevices, but rather in the middle of the leaf undersides, and often oozes droplets of a clear sticky substance. Unfortunately the sticky masses protect the scales from the parasite *Encarsia*, so this method of control is not effective. The only method of control other than using chemical spray is to wash all sticky patches off with a soapy solution and spray the adults with the same, preferably early in the morning when they are least active.

Aphids

More commonly known as 'greenflies' they can be green, black or brownish. They sit on stems, leaves and buds, sucking juices out of the plant, thus debilitating it and possibly introducing virus diseases.

Their numbers suddenly explode from a few, to millions, and appear as soon as there is a little warmth in the early spring weather. Aphids are easy to kill with chemicals or soap sprays, but they do keep reappearing so constant vigilance is required. An easier method of control is to introduce one or two natural predators early in the season, which will seek out aphids as they come in from outside, dealing with them before they become a problem. One of the pest controllers required for aphids is *Aphidius*. This is a little midge-like 'wasp' which occurs naturally outdoors in the UK and very often finds it's own way into greenhouses and conservatories. It lays it's eggs into live aphids. The young then develop, using the aphids as food, turning it into a golden-brown crispened shell or 'mummy' out of which it bites a hole, emerging as an adult to start the cycle again.

The *Aphidius* are very mobile and move about between batches of plants seeking out their prey, giving very effective results within only a few weeks.

Aphidolites is another useful predator for aphids. This is a predatory midge, whose larvae feed on several species in low light conditions and at night. One larvae may eat between 4 and 65 aphids a day depending on the size of the aphid.

Mealybug
This is a small white, woodlice shaped insect which invades a wide range of host plants, unfortunately this includes citrus. It tends to be found under leaves and in nooks and crannies and leaf joints. It sucks sap from the tree, weakening it and excreting honeydew which attracts sooty mould. There are several species of mealybug, but the one that is generally found in the UK greenhouses and conservatories is *Planococcus Citri* (citrus mealybug).

Females lay up to 600 eggs over 8-10 days on cotton-wool like masses. These hatch in about 10 days, releasing crawlers which spread over the plant and live for 1-6 months depending on temperature. Soap sprays are reasonably effective as long as every last bug is found, and as long as the spray can penetrate the cotton wool masses. It may be better to use a soapy sponge to wash the tree clean.

The pest controller for mealybug is a brown Australian ladybird called *Cryptolaemus Montrouzieri* which thrives on bad infestations. It eats all stages of mealybugs and will also feed on aphids and immature scale insects if mealybugs are in short supply. These ladybirds have to be introduced during the evening when they can readily find their food and will not fly away until no more food can be found, otherwise they have a habit of disappearing, particularly if introduced on a bright sunny day when they will just fly up to the roof and probably out of the windows and doors. The offspring of the *Cryptolaemus* look very much like mealybugs when they are in certain stages of development, so care must be taken when pruning not to remove them or kill them by mistake. *Cryptolaemus Montrouzieri* lay their eggs in the cottony masses of mealybug eggs. Their eggs hatch in 5-10 days and the

150

following larval stage, during which the larvae suck out the body contents of eggs and young nymphs of mealybugs, lasts between 12-24 days when temperatures exceed 21°C (70°F). There is a subsequent white pupal stage, taking the total time of development from egg to next generation of egg, to 33-54 days, when temperatures are above 21°C. It is the larval stage which resembles the mealybugs, so care must be taken not to destroy the *Cryptolaemus Montrouzieri* at this stage.

Temperatures above 21°C (70°F) favour *Cryptolaemus,* so control during the winter months will be limited. They feed heavily, so small numbers can be adequate to control quite a large outbreak of mealybug in sufficiently warm temperatures.

Some control can also be achieved with *Leptomastix Dactylopii*, which is a short yellowish-brown 'wasp'. This is effective only with *Planococcus Citri*, not with other species of mealybug, so accurate identification of the pest is important. It is less readily available than *Cryptolaemus,* but may be worth a try if the other control seems to be ineffective.

Scale Insect.
There are many different species of scale insect, all of which can severely debilitate plants and citrus trees if left unchecked. They are little brown warts or oval scales generally on the stems and underside of leaves, sucking sap and depositing large amounts of sticky honeydew on leaves underneath the infestations.

There are soft scale insects and armoured scales, both of which can be kept in check with soap sprays, provided that all leaf and stem surfaces are covered, and that the larger scales are rubbed off at the time so that any eggs lurking underneath can also be touched by the spray.

A female may harbour as many as 2000 eggs, which when hatched, crawl around the tree looking for suitable sites on which to settle. They then go through a further two growth stages before becoming adults.

Armoured scale is difficult to control by parasitic insects, but soft scales can be controlled by *Metaphycus Helvolus.*

Metaphycus Helvolus is a tiny parasitic, pale coloured 'wasp' which both sucks the juices out of the adult scale insects and lays eggs in others which are in the first and second stages of development. It requires temperatures above 21°C to be properly active, and at it's peak may kill 25 scale insects a day. Unfortunately *Metaphycus Helvolus* is very difficult to produce and supplies can therefore be unreliable.

Caterpillar

Caterpillars tend to be a problem only in the summer months, and although they are not generally health threatening, they can disfigure the plant considerably by curling the leaves, in which they make a nest, and eating the leaves, the flower buds and the fruit. Keep a close eye on any part of the tree that appears to be stuck together, take off the leaf or seek out the offender.

The main culprit is the Tortrix moth, but any flying insect that produces leaf eating caterpillars could also find a home on your tree. The most sure biological control for this is *Bacillus Thuringiensis*, a powder which mixes with water and is sprayed onto the leaves. The caterpillars ingest the spray as they eat the leaves and then gradually die over a period of days.

Another method of caterpillar control is to catch the moths and butterflies before they can lay their eggs. There are moth catching lights, but these also tend to attract *Aphidius* and other beneficial flying insects. You can buy pheromone traps, which can be very effective provided you can accurately match the pheromone lure to the type of moth that is causing the problem. The traps work by imitating the natural pheromone attractant of the insects, to lure and trap them.

Vine Weevil

These are little beetles, about 75 mm long that chew notches out of the edges of leaves. The really damaging part of their life cycle is when their eggs hatch into grubs in the compost around the plants, including citrus. The grubs voraciously eat their way through the roots of the plant, leaving the plant stem totally disconnected from it's root system.

Vine weevils are an increasing problem having invaded many gardens, greenhouses and conservatories. They are difficult to control by conventional means, however there is a biological control in the form of nematodes, or eel worms. These can be bought in different forms, suspended in gel or in sponges. They are watered into the compost and they kill the grubs within a couple of weeks. There is no control for adult weevils, so it is best to make several applications of nematodes while conditions are warm enough, to catch the succession of developing grubs.

Warmth is the great limitation of nematodes, they only work if the compost temperature is above 15°C (60°F) and for only 2 weeks after application. This limits outdoor use to June, July and August, although in conservatories they can be used for as long as the required temperature can be maintained. The compost must be moist before application and must remain damp for two weeks afterwards to keep the nematodes active. Citrus tree compost should never be allowed to dry out, so this precaution should not be a problem.

If you know that you have a vine-weevil problem in your garden, then as a precaution at the introduction of new citrus trees, cover the compost completely with a layer of coconut matting or suitable material that will allow water to pass through, but keep the vine-weevils out, preventing the adults laying eggs in the compost. This can be disguised with a layer of grit or stones or any attractive similar looking product to finish off, effectively trying to seal the compost from the beetles.

Ants

Ants are usually after honey-dew produced by leaf sucking pests, or in some cases the pests themselves. Control of the pest should mean the ants will disappear, but if they have nested in the compost, wash the tree with soap and water, to remove all trace of pests and honey-dew on that particular tree, carefully removing any biological control that may be in situ to another site and if necessary use an ant killing jelly as a band around the trunk of the tree and on the edge of the pot.

The decision to go *Biological* is quite a major one and at first may seem rather daunting. You have to remember that you cannot revert back to spraying chemicals without the risk of killing the beneficial insects. The other point to remember is that citrus trees should be outside in the summer and brought in, in the winter to the conservatory or greenhouse.

During the winter you can get quite high temperatures under glass and pest control of some sort is essential. Outside, keeping your 'pest controllers' in the vicinity of your citrus tree may be a problem. Biological pest control therefore is generally used in greenhouses and conservatories that are kept at above 6°C (40°F) in winter, but for warmer conservatories the season for use of beneficial insects is prolonged. If you maintain a controlled temperature of 15°C (60°F) then biological control will be year-round.

So for those who find that washing an entire tree with soapy water is too time consuming, and spraying with chemicals is not for you, then using a range of different biological controls, applied only after the pests become evident, may be easier, cleaner, more effective and kinder to you and the environment.

LEAF FALL

Citrus trees are **deciduous trees** and have to shed their leaves annually, but unlike British native species, they usually do not shed their leaves until after the new leaves appear. Citrus trees, mainly lemons, have a habit of shedding their leaves and looking bare and unattractive for what appears to be 'no-reason'. Don't be tempted to cut the tree back drastically. This is not necessary as the new growth will appear when you have corrected the problem.

Leaf loss early in Winter. Some leaf loss will occur when the trees are first brought inside. It may take 3-4 weeks for the tree to adapt to the change of environment. The main cause is **underfeeding**, particularly lack of nitrogen. You may have been feeding your tree, but excessive watering caused by weather conditions may have had the effect of washing out the nutrients from the compost. To help prevent this, cover the pot with a polythene apron during long periods of rainy weather and give extra feeds using the summer food (higher nitrogen formula) as soon as the tree is brought inside, until the loss stops. The change of humidity levels is also a cause of stress. Spray the tree a lot when first brought inside to acclimatise the tree to the new conditions.

Leaf loss is also seen when a tree has been constantly fed on a **high potash food** produced for tomatoes or house-plants. There is insufficient nitrogen to sustain the leaf growth.

As the tree requires less water in the winter there may be a danger of underfeeding in an effort not to over-water or produce excessive humidity. A light sprinkling of winter food directly on the compost which is then watered in, or doubling the quantity mixed with the water may help.

If the tree stops taking up water in the winter it is a sign that it has become dormant and this will lead to loss of leaves. It is usually caused by **very low night temperatures**, so raise the night temperature either by covering the tree at night with bubble insulation film or polythene, or improving the heating using a thermostatically controlled heater. When the tree starts taking up water again, it will also be taking up food and will then start to re-grow it's leaves.

Over acidity can also cause leaf loss, especially if Sulphate of Ammonia has been used to feed the tree, but this is shown on the leaves by a browning along the centre of the leaf, spreading towards the outside. Correcting the pH with lime may help to save the tree, but be sure of the facts first before you start to add lime.

Lack of humidity is a crucial factor in leaf loss, especially if your tree is kept in a centrally heated room in winter. Spray the tree regularly if kept in these conditions, and if possible take the tree outside occasionally and give a really good hose down. It may be necessary to consider an indoor waterfall, if the alternatives prove too difficult. Light stress may also be a contributory factor. If this is the case try using a 'grow-lamp' on the tree to improve the lighting.

Leaf loss in Summer is generally a sign that the roots are being scorched or are drying out. Standing your tree on a hot sun terrace, particularly if it is sheltered with very little air movement, may be the cause. Sometimes the temperature in these areas can be excessive, a real 'sun-trap'. The tree is literally burning up. Place the pot into a secondary pot containing peat or stones at the base and keep this moist. Water the tree well, improve the feeding programme and spray the tree to keep the leaves fresh. If possible transfer the tree to a more shady spot.

Citrus trees kept in the conservatory for the summer may also suffer the same fate, accentuated by being near the glass. Keep your trees near the back of the conservatory away from the glass and raise the humidity, either by frequent spraying or by using an indoor waterfall. Shading may also be necessary to keep the temperature down and good ventilation will be essential.

YELLOWING LEAVES

This is usually a sign of trace element deficiency. Each trace element, or the lack of the element, produces a different discolouration on the leaf, so can be identified, but our special fertilizers have all the trace elements the tree requires and should correct any deficiencies. If the tree has been grossly underfed, then use the fertilizer at every watering or in the winter use at double strength until the tree recovers, reducing then to once a week or normal dosage.

The fertilizer can be used as a foliar spray, but the blue dye contained in the fertilizer may mark the leaves. This is only surface marking, it is not damaging to the leaf and could be washed off. It should not be necessary to give any other supplements to the tree. New shoots absorb trace elements more readily than the older leaves, so always ensure a good foliar feed when the tree is actively producing new growth. At the same time continue with root feeding which is always needed.

If you have been feeding your tree, but still have yellowing leaves, the cause may be a pH problem. If the pH goes out of range from 6.5 - 7, the tree cannot absorb half the iron you may be feeding it and two thirds of the magnesium. It may even be that the pot is now too small and the tree cannot absorb enough food, or possibly that the roots have been damaged by over watering or infestation. If necessary, **re-pot the tree into a John Innes No 3, or a specialist citrus compost with the correct pH of 6.5, at the same time prune back the tree to stimulate new growth and re-shape.** The leaf colour should be three times darker on the top than the underside. If the tree is full of fruit, less food will be going into the leaves and they will be lighter in colour.

FRUIT DROP OR PREMATURE RIPENING OF IMMATURE FRUITS

Until we started issuing our growing instructions, the only available information in Britain regarding the feeding of container grown citrus trees was that they should be given **high potash foods** from April to October and not fed at all in the winter. With citrus trees blossoming in the winter and early spring, this had the effect of producing a very weak tree which would flower profusely or not flower at all. The profuse flowering was generally followed by the complete collapse of the tree, or at the least, a massive amount of fruit drop.

The trees have to be fed in the winter to build up the strength needed to produce blossom and fruit, and nitrogen is needed to set the fruit and bring the fruits to their full size, not potash. Using our special fertilizers for citrus trees will correct this problem.

Other factors causing fruit drop are **excessive temperatures** when the tree is in blossom and **inadequate watering** during this time. It has to be recognised that the tree will produce a great number of blossoms, not all of which will set fruit. The tree will shed any fruit it cannot hold, so attention to temperature, watering and feeding during the winter and spring is the best encouragement and support for heavy crops. It is not necessary to thin out the fruitlets.

Making The Most Of Citrus

CITRUS AND THE HONEY BEE

Citrus trees do not require the services of bees as they set fruit without pollination, infact many varieties do not contain viable pollen. This is called *parenthocarpy*. The bees however very much appreciate the nectar and pollen produced by citrus trees. It makes an excellent honey, pale in colour with a mild taste, taking on the flavour of the plant itself.

Although made from the nectar of a variety of different oranges, lemons, limes, mandarins and grapefruits, the honey is usually referred to as 'Orange Blossom Honey'.

Bee hives are as much of a tradition in the Citrus Groves as the trees themselves, but the honey is usually sold to a co-operative, blended and sold on from there.

Honey is as old as civilization itself, it's importance has been chronicled throughout history, even early cave drawings depict man's attempt to obtain honeycombs from beehives. The Ancient Greeks thought honey was the food of the Gods, and in Saxon Britain it was even used to pay taxes.

Over the years, man has developed thousands of uses for honey, in food, drinks, medicine and cosmetics. However no scientist has ever succeeded in manufacturing an artificial honey that matches up to nature's original and we still rely on honey bees to make it for us.

Bees make honey from the nectar of blossoms as a food store for the winter months. Honey is a pure and natural food, it contains no additives, it's flavour, aroma and texture depend on such diverse things as the soil, the plant origin and the climate. Some honeys taste sweeter than others and the colour of honey can range from the near white of clover honey to the very dark brown of horse-chestnut honey.

We know that honey is made of different sugars, mainly fructose and glucose and small amounts of vitamins and proteins. Honey is rapidly absorbed into the blood-stream as the sugars have already been 'broken down' by the bees, and so it provides instant energy for the body.

There are several species of honey bee, but it is the European honey bee or hive bee *(apis mellifera)* which makes most of the world's honey. The organisation of the colony is both incredibly efficient and complex.

A typical honey bee colony contains around 50,000 bees plus larvae and eggs. All the activity centres around the queen bee. The queen is larger than the other bees and her main job is to lay eggs, as many as 2,000 a day. Indeed, she may produce a million eggs in her lifetime. The workers feed the queen bee with royal jelly, which is a highly nutritious milky white fluid made by the glands in their head. The workers' diet is pollen and nectar.

Drones are the only males in the hive. There are usually no more than 300 of them and they are heavily built, have large eyes and make the famous droning noise. The drones' job is to mate with the queen bee.

It is workers who perform most of the tasks in the colony. They are the smallest honey bees and make up about 98% of the total, that is around 50,000. Their bodies are constructed for maximum efficiency. Their hind legs have hairs to hold pollen. They have a tongue to suck nectar and mandibles to defend the colony and to chew wax for building the comb. This is produced from special glands under their abdomens. The workers only sting if they are approached or harmed. However, by using their sting they will die, unlike wasps.

As well as gathering nectar to make honey, the workers care for the eggs and larvae in the hives, build combs, feed the queen bee and guard the colony against intruders.

In the hive, worker bees build combs of beeswax where they raise the young larvae and store food. Honeycombs are miracles of engineering and design and are made of six sided cells. Each comb is two cells thick. All the cells have a slight backward tilt so the honey won't spill out.

Plant nectar, the bee's main food, is found in the blossom. The honey bees suck up the liquid from the nectaries of the flower and store it in their stomachs where it is mixed with enzymes and gradually turned into a honey-like fluid. They pass the 'honey' to the hive workers who complete the honey making process by depositing the honey in the honeycomb cells and fanning it with their wings to reduce the moisture content. When the cell is full it is capped with beeswax.

Pollen is a fine dusty material you see on the stamens of flowers. As the forager bees search for nectar the pollen gets stuck on their bodies. They bring the pollen back to the hive and pass it to the house workers who knead it with nectar to make 'bee bread' to feed to the young bees.

In the early days, man used to raid wild bee colonies to obtain honey.

The first bee hives were hollow logs, discarded baskets or clay pots that bees happened to settle in. Then man built hives out of clay, wicker or wood, the old English straw 'skep' was an example. The trouble was that the nest within has to be broken up to get the honey out. One of the greatest changes in bee-keeping was in 1851 when a Philadelphian minister, Lorenzo Lorraine Langstroth invented a moveable frame hive. This was a square wooden hive with vertical frames which could be pulled out to check the colony.

Nowadays when honeycomb in the hive is filled with honey, it is taken from the hive and brought to an existing plant called a 'honey house'. The wax cappings are removed with a steam heated knife and then the honeycomb is placed in revolving baskets where the spinning movement throws out the honey by centrifugal force. Extracting the honey in this way does harm to the hive, which the bees repair, polishing each cell ready for a new load.

The honey is strained and left to stand until air bubbles rise, then skimmed, after which it is ready for bottling.

As well as engineers, worker bees are also navigators. When searching for nectar they can cover as many as thirty square miles. By using the sun as a compass, they can not only find their way back to the hive, they can also tell the other bees where to find the nectar.

The bees perform a 'round dance' when the food source is nearby which lets the other bees know the taste and smell of the nectar. The 'waggle dance' is more complicated and is performed when the food is more than 100 meters away. The direction of the waggle determines the position of the food source in relation to the sun.

The ancient Greeks loved honey, it was part of their mythology. They thought that it fell from the skies and called it Ambrosia, the food of the gods. Nectar, the drink of the gods, was another name for mead (a drink made from honey).

In the Roman Empire, honey production was an important business, one of their sacrificial cakes 'Libum' was made with honey.

The Arabians have a proverb in their philosophy about life: "Yuam asal, Yuam basal..." (Some days it's honey, some days it's onions).

In Greece, a newly wedded girl was given a spoonful of honey by her mother-in-law, so only sweet words would pass her lips during married life.

Britain has been famed for it's honey. When the Phoenicians arrived to trade in copper and tin, they called Britain "The Isle of Honey".

In Britain, mead was a common drink for several thousand years. Medieval writers said "There is no drink which conduceth more to the preservation of one".

Saxon Lords of the manor accepted honey as part payment for rents due. Swarms of bees used to be given as gifts or dowries.

Bees were kept in monasteries as monks used beeswax to make candles.

Did You Know?
Honey is a mild antiseptic. It's anti-bacterial properties are helped by it's high sugar content.

Honey has hygroscopic properties, it attracts and retains moisture and so is widely used in beauty products as a skin softener and hair conditioner.

Bees are important pollinators. They are often rented by fruit growers to help pollinate their orchards in the spring.

To produce 1 lb of honey it is estimated that honey bees have to travel a distance equivalent to three times around the world, that is about 90,000 miles.

The worker bee carries almost her own weight in nectar, an amazing feat of aerodynamics.

If you are stung by a bee, do not attempt to squeeze out the sting as this forces the poison further in. Gently pull the sting out with tweezers.

Honey comes from all over the world, but the sunnier countries produce more as the flowers grow richer for longer in a warm climate.

British bees cannot produce enough honey for everyone, so honey is imported, mainly from Mexico, Australia and China. Russia and America also produce large amounts of honey.

Honey keeps for a very long time and never goes off. A jar of Egyptian honey was found in a tomb at the beginning of this century and although the honey was discoloured, it still kept it's taste and scent after over 3,000 years.

All honey crystalises or sets after a time. If it is cold it will crystallize more quickly, so clear honey should never be kept in a refrigerator. If you warm the crystallized honey, it will become clear again.

Colds and 'Flu

Honey and lemon as a combination has always been a traditional remedy for cold and 'flu symptoms.

2 tablespoons of orange blossom honey
1 tablespoon of lemon juice
a little menthol or eucalyptus oil

Add ingredients to a glass of hot water to help sooth away the symptoms. For the adults, a little whisky added will help you to relax and sleep better.

CITRUS FOR HEALTH AND VITAMIN C

The history of Vitamin C is quite interesting. Vitamin C deficiency or 'Scurvy' was first described in 1500 BC in the 'Ebers Papyrus'. Hypocrates, instigator of the Doctors' Hyppocratic Oath also described an illness amongst large numbers of soldiers which showed symptoms involving leg pains, gangrene of the gums and loss of teeth. During the Crusades, more men died of scurvy than were killed by the Saracens.

Maggellan a famous Portuguese sailor who circumnavigated the world and who gave his name to the Maggellan Straights in South America is said to have lost 90% of his crew to Scurvy.

During the winter of 1555, Jacques Cartiers mounted an expedition in Canada during which 100 of the 110 men he took with him suffered from Scurvy. They were successfully treated by an infusion of swamp spruce leaves which contained Vitamin C. This was the first recorded treatment of Scurvy.

James Lind wrote "A Treatise on the Scurvy" in 1757 in which he described his experiments on the prevention and cure of the disease. He found that orange and lemon juice were the most effective. It took nearly 50 years for the Royal Navy to act on this information but in 1804 it decreed a daily ration of lemon or lime juice to each sailor thus earning them the nickname of 'limeys'. The improved health of the sailors was to prove crucial in the naval battles of the Napoleonic wars.

The modern study of Scurvy started as it were by accident. In 1907 Holst and Frolich were attempting to induce beri-beri in the guinea pigs they were studying, and caused them to suffer with scurvy. This was quite fortunate, as guinea pigs are one of the few animals (besides man) who are unable to synthesize their own Vitamin C.

In 1928 Albert Szent Gyorgyi isolated an acidic carbohydrate from cabbage, lemon juice and adrenal glands. He knew that it was related to sugars but not which one. He called the new sugar 'ignose', after 'ignosco' which means 'don't know' and 'ose' which means 'sugar'. His suggestion was not greeted kindly by the editor of the Biochemical Journal, a man who was not noted for his sense of humour. A second suggestion of 'godnose' received a similarly stony reception. It was eventually called 'hexuronic acid' as the compound had six carbon atoms and was acidic. However Szent Gyorgyi made no connection between his newly isolated compound and the anti-scorbutic substance found in citrus fruits first described by Lind.

In 1932 Waugh and King isolated the anti-scorbutic factor in lemon juice and showed that it was the same as hexuronic acid. The name ascorbic acid was adopted in recognition of the biological activity of the compound as the anti-scorbutic factor.

Vitamin C is essential for the formation of collagen, ground substance, osteoid, dentine and inter-cellular cement substance.

Collagen is the substance that provides the framework for many of the important tissues in the body. Specifically it provides the framework for bone, blood-vessels serving the teeth, and tendons. Without the presence of Vitamin C the chemical processes involved in the formation of collagen cannot take place. When this happens, bone, teeth blood-vessels and tendons cannot be properly made and the person suffers from defects involving these structures. These are the symptoms associated with scurvy.

Vitamin C is also important for the preservation and maturation of fibroplasts which are the cells which lay down collagen tissue and form a crucial part of the wound healing process.

Vitamin C has an essential role to play in the elaboration of two of the twenty essential amino-acids required for a healthy body. Other amino-acids requiring Vitamin C have a role to play in the nervous system, amongst other places. The presence of large quantities of Vitamin C in the human cortex also suggests Vitamin C may have an important part in the formation and release of cortico-steroids which are vitally important in the body's response to shock, injury and infection. Cortico-steroids also have roles to play in the metabolism of other minerals and carbohydrates.

There have been a number of reports which show a low Vitamin C status in patients with advanced cancer. For example, Krasner and Dymock showed that in 46 out of 50 patients with a variety of malignant tumours, their Vitamin C content was below the normal minimum value. Further studies demonstrated that increasing the amounts of Vitamin C in patients with advanced cancer was associated with increased longevity and lessening of the more distressing symptoms.

This may be because a number of tumours accumulate relatively large amounts of Vitamin C at the expense of the surrounding normal tissue and hence ultimately at the expense of the patient. By giving patients large amounts of Vitamin C, in excess of 1000mg per day, this process is cancelled and the patient as a result does better.

There is also some evidence to suggest that large amounts of Vitamin C prevent the absorption in the body of potentially cancer causing chemicals. Much work is still under way.

In 1974 Cameron and Pauling published a view suggesting that there was an enhancement of host resistance to cancer in patients with high levels of Vitamin C. Specifically they suggested that patients with terminal cancer seemed to live longer if the Vitamin C status was normal. There was also a suggestion by Pauling that the presence of high doses of Vitamin C about the body make a stronger type of collagen which was more resistant to invasive tumours.

Basu and his co-workers showed that in patients with bony metastases, secondary to breast cancer (but not in other patients) there was a considerable reduction in the bone pain when the patients were given one gram of Vitamin C per day. Other studies however have not been quite as positive in their results and there remains some controversy about the role of Vitamin C in cancer.

Linus Pauling, who has twice been awarded the Nobel Prize for Physics, and is one of the most respected scientists alive, has worked on the role of Vitamin C since 1970. He related the role of Vitamin C in the prevention of the common cold in a paper written in the 1970's. He suggested that doses of one gram per day of Vitamin C helped prevent the common cold. Further studies however have shown that large doses of Vitamin C does not prevent the incidence of common cold, but the sufferer manifests fewer symptoms in the duration of the illness, than those who do not take Vitamin C. This may be because the general draining effect of the illness is reversed by adding Vitamin C (as in patients with cancer) or that the addition of Vitamin C has a beneficial effect on cell mediated immune response. Unfortunately this effect has not been demonstrated convincingly in humans.

There is some controversy as to exactly how much Vitamin C is required to maintain health in the human body. Estimates range from 30mg per day for adults, to as high as 75mg per day. This is because one study recommended the dose necessary to prevent scurvy, and another study in a different country recommended a dose sufficient to prevent a depletion of tissue saturation (the level of Vitamin C in the blood and tissues). A generally agreed figure would be between 45 and 60mgs of Vitamin C per day. This is based on the estimation of the average amount of Vitamin C in the human body and the amount that is used daily. An average western diet normally includes more than sufficient Vitamin C to maintain an adequate level.

The role of citrus fruit is, as already historically established, important in assuring that this level is maintained. For example, 100ml of fresh orange juice contains between 70-105mgs of Vitamin C. This is more than sufficient for the average daily requirement. However it is important to note that any processing of food (cooking, heating, freezing) alters the Vitamin C content drastically. Apple juice which is a rich source of Vitamin C loses it's Vitamin C content extremely rapidly as soon as it is stored. Within 24 hours the vast majority of Vitamin C present in apple juice is gone. This is because the presence of oxygen in the environment causes Vitamin C to undergo a chemical change (oxidation) which effectively neutralizes it. Storing apple juice in an oxygen free environment slows oxidation and keeps the Vitamin C content relatively constant.

Citrus juices, such as orange and lemon juices, also lose their Vitamin C content fairly rapidly, but not as rapidly as apple juice. It is important to realize that fresh fruits such as an orange will supply the normal daily requirement, but if this has been stored in any form outside the natural fruit (without proper processing) the Vitamin C content can be drastically reduced.

Processing food, such as cooking, virtually ensures that natural Vitamin C is destroyed. Therefore it is important to have an adequate intake of fresh Vitamin C from source, such as citrus fruits to ensure an adequate supply. It should be noted however that many processed foods have added Vitamin C in the form of ascorbic acid, and that this supply having been added, the Vitamin C content remains fairly constant.

To summarize, it appears that Vitamin C levels in the human body are easily maintained by regular intake of foods rich in Vitamin C such as citrus fruits. There is increasing evidence that adequate levels of Vitamin C have a protective effect against cancer and some infections.

CITRUS ESSENTIAL OILS

Plants have always provided natural solutions not only for health but also for beauty. They have been used in many forms since time began, even animals choose to eat different plants as part of their own requirement for treatment.

All parts of the plant may be used, but not necessarily all parts of the same plant. Extractions called 'Essential Oils' are yielded from flowers, leaves, seeds, fruits, bark and roots.

Citrus yield essential oils from the flowers, unripe fruits, peel of ripe fruits, leaves, bark and twigs. Most of the oils are extracted by steam distillation, or solvents, but the citrus fruits yield their oils from cold pressing of the peel by hand or machine.

Essential oils may vary in consistency and can be watery or thick, but they are not greasy. They can be mixed in vegetable oils and readily dissolve in alcohol, but they do not dissolve in water.

The colours of essential oils have a wide range, dependent on their source. They can be yellow, orange, red, green, brown, blue or just colourless. The fragrance also varies and may be fruity, musky, woody, spicy, minty or floral.

CITRUS IN AROMATHERAPY

Citrus oils play an important, although small part in Aromatherapy, and their oils, particularly the neroli oil are much prized. All the citrus essential oils are used, but as with all oils, they are never used in isolation.

Aromatherapists use their skills and knowledge to prepare combinations of essential oils for therapy or treatment, bringing maximum benefit to the recipient.

Essential oils have the ability to regulate the metabolism and balance the mind and body, stimulating the memory and the emotions. They readily permeate the whole body, in many different ways, by inhalation, vaporization or by skin penetration through massage,

167

bathing, compress or application, and travel the blood stream and the lymphatic system to bring healing, cleansing, detoxifying, invigorating, relaxing or rejuvenating benefits. They have antiseptic, anti-bacterial, anti-inflammatory, anti-fungal and expectorant, diuretic, and a host of other properties. Some essential oils benefit specific organs while others have a more general effect.

The total of the essential oils used in one bottle should not be more than 2% mixed with a base oil, but for treating children, a 1% dilution is recommended. They should never be used undiluted because being extremely effective, they can also be very toxic if taken in excess. The base oil itself can be particular to the treatment being given. Essential oil treatments are mixed as required and used immediately. They have a short shelf life.

BITTER ORANGE
citrus aurantium

The bitter orange, Naranja Amarga and other similar varieties grow mainly in Morocco, Algeria, Egypt, Italy, Spain and also in Southern France, where they are grown in plantations specifically for the harvest of flowers. This profusion of blossom is then hand picked just as the flowers are about to open. It is collected first thing in the morning, two or three times a week during May. The tree will produce blossom from three years old and will not reach full maturity until it is twenty years old, when it will produce an average of 50 - 60 lbs of blossoms.

In mild and favourable autumnal conditions, the tree will bear a second harvest which may last until January, or until touched by frost, but the oil is not valued at the same price as the spring blossom because the perfume is not as strong. The yield of oil is greatly affected by the temperature and conditions prevailing at the time of harvest.

The flowers are subject to steam distillation and produce the much prized pale yellow Neroli Oil. This is used extensively in the high class perfume industry, but is also used in aromatherapy.

The perfume of this oil is very distinctive with a combination of fragrances, sweet, fruity, spicy and bitter. It was named after a Princess of Nerola in Italy who loved to wear it as a perfume. It's use in aromatherapy is related to the hypnotic effect it has on the mind, which makes it especially suitable for the treatment of insomnia. It has a calming effect on the nervous system and is therefore used for the treatment of depression and anxiety, as well as for relieving stress or shock. It is useful for the treatment of pre-menstrual tension (PMT).

The heart is calmed by the action of neroli oil and so it's use extends to those who are sensitive, apprehensive or alarmed. It was traditionally used as a bridal bouquet to calm the nerves of the bride on her wedding day, and also acts as an aphrodisiac.

Neroli oil has regenerative powers, promoting cell growth, and is used on areas of broken capillaries, scars, stretch marks, and when used on the face it helps to reduce wrinkles and improve dry skin. It has antiseptic, bactericidal and fungicidal properties, and is an effective deodorant.

The anti-spasmodic effects of the oil will calm the digestive system and is therefore used to treat diarrhoea, colic, flatulence and nervous dyspepsia. In parts of Europe, an infusion of orange blossom is used as a mild stimulant of the nervous system and as a blood cleanser.

The fruit of the bitter orange is used for the production of Orange Bitter Oil, also called Oil of Bigarade. The oil is cold-pressed from the peel of the orange by hand or by machine. It has a typical odour of oranges, is lively, bright, bitter and dry and used in the perfume industry. It is used extensively to bring out the freshness in what is referred to in the industry as 'top notes'.

In aromatherapy it's uses are the same as for sweet orange oil.

The bitter orange tree also yields an essential oil from steam distillation of the leaves and twigs. This is known as Petitgrain Oil. The fragrance of this oil is difficult to describe, being both sweet and bitter, a floral, citrus scent, with a slight woody note. It is used in the perfume industry, and is one of the traditional ingredients of eau-de-cologne.

It gets it's name from the fact that at one time the oil was extracted from the small unripe fruits, or *petit-grains*. It forms the familiar fragrance found in soaps and detergents, is used in the cosmetic industry, and is also an important ingredient in confectionery, in alcohol and in soft drinks.

In aromatherapy is it used for it's astringent properties which tone and balance the skin, so is used to treat acne, excessive perspiration, and greasy skin and hair. It benefits the nervous system, having a calming effect on the mind, and is therefore helpful in relieving anxiety, palpitations, insomnia and nervous exhaustion. It also has a calming effect on the digestive system and is used to treat dyspepsia and flatulence.

SWEET ORANGE
citrus sinensis

There are several ways the essential oils can be expressed from the sweet orange. It can be produced from cold-pressing the peel and producing an oil golden yellow in colour and with a fragrance typical of oranges, lively, sweet and fruity; by distillation of the peel, and by distillation of the essences produced after orange juice has been extracted. The oil produced from distillation is much lighter in colour and has a lighter, sweet, fruity scent. The flowers also yield an essential oil called neroli petalae or neroli Portugal, and a small amount of oil may be produced from the leaves.

It is used extensively in the perfume industry and in cosmetics as well as forming the fragrance in soaps and detergents. Medicines are flavoured with tincture, produced from the sweet orange peel.

The aromatherapist will use sweet orange oil to stimulate the digestive and lymphatic systems, improving conditions of obesity and water retention, also relieving constipation and dyspepsia. It can also be used as a treatment to improve the appetite and the general well being of the digestive tract. As with other orange oils, the calming effect it has on the body can be harnassed in the treatment of nervous tension and other stress related conditions. It will act as an anti-depressant.

Sweet orange oil also has a warming effect on the body and is used for the treatment of colds and 'flu, bronchitis and chills. It has antiseptic and bactericidal properties which can be used to relieve mouth ulcers. It has a refreshing effect on dull and also oily skin conditions.

Although generally non-toxic, there are large amounts of a chemical called limonene present in sweet orange oil which has been known to cause dermatitis in some people, also the distilled orange oil, as distinct from the cold-pressed oil, is phototoxic so should not be used on the skin prior to sun-bathing.

170

BERGAMOT ORANGE
citrus bergamia

Bergamot produces a light greenish yellow oil from the cold-pressed peel and unripe fruits, which is a delicate but refreshing sweet, fruity, citrus fragrance. The name of Bergamot comes from the city of Bergamo in Italy where it was first sold, being a treatment for fever and for worms. Bergamot oil is now known to have an extensive range of applications.

The antiseptic properties of bergamot oil are used to treat mouth infections, including sore throat and tonsillitis, as well as halitosis. Genito-urinary infections such as cystitis and thrush, amongst others, can also be treated. Bergamot oil stimulates the immune system and so helps to treat colds, 'flu, and infectious diseases.

The uplifting effect of bergamot oil is used to treat anxiety, depression and stress related conditions including loss of appetite.

Bergamot oil is also used as a treatment for many skin conditions such as psoriasis, herpes, eczema, acne, shingles, ulcers and wounds as well as scabies, but the areas treated should not be exposed to sunlight after treatment as there are chemicals contained in bergamot oil that are phototoxic and which therefore may cause sensitization of the skin and skin pigmentation. However, Bergamot oil is used extensively in the cosmetic, toiletries, suntan and perfume industries, as well as in the food industry and is a notable ingredient in Earl Grey tea.

MANDARIN
citrus reticulata

Mandarins yield an essential oil from the peel which has a finer and sweeter fragrance than the oranges, is refreshingly lively and almost exotic. It is a very important component in the perfume industry, being used in what is termed 'fantasy perfumes' and it is used in the food industry as a flavouring agent in sweets, soft drinks and liqueurs.

A small amount of petitgrain oil can be produced from steam distillation of the leaves and twigs.

In aromatherapy mandarin oil is used for it's calming and soothing effect on the nervous and digestive systems. This oil is one of the few that is safe to use by, and beneficial for, the pregnant mother. It is mild enough to be used to treat children, having anti-spasmodic properties, it is used for hiccoughs and dyspepsia, and it's sedative properties calm restlessness, insomnia and nervous tension. It is also good for troublesome oily skin. It's toning qualities can be used to treat fluid retention and obesity.

LEMON

citrus medica or citrus limon

The essential oil from lemons is the most widely known and perhaps the most widely used with familiar healing properties.

It has a very lively refreshing odour and is found in many brands of products commonly available for the consumer. In the manufacture of perfumes, it is a classic oil and used mainly in what is known as 'fantasy perfumes'.

The tangy fresh fragrance of the lemon oil invigorates even the taste buds, regulates the stomach acidity, relieving gastritis and indigestion, stimulating the immune system and enhancing the body's ability to resist infection. It is very useful in the treatment of cold and 'flu symptoms and easing sore throats and so it is found in many prepared cold remedies.

In aromatherapy, lemon oil is used for it's astringent and tonic action on the body, toning the circulatory system, regulating body fluids and reducing water retention. It is also used in the treatment of cellulite, a problem many women are familiar with.

Lemon oil can be used to improve spotty and oily skins and is even used for bleaching freckles. Other skin problems such as warts, verrucas and corns can be treated with lemon oil.

LIME

citrus aurantifolia

Lime oil can be obtained from either steam distillation of the crushed unripe fruit or by cold pressing the peel of the ripe fruits. It has many similarities of lemon with a very intense lively sweet odour which is used as a freshener in perfumes.

It's use in aromatherapy and medicine is the same as for lemons and the choice for it's use would be by preference only.

Items from the 'Prince of Neroli' range of Products
'Cosmetics to Go'

CITRUS
FOR BEAUTY AND COSMETICS

The emphasis to-day is on wholesome natural products that have not been cruelly tested on animals. A Dorset company 'Cosmetics to Go' specializes in beauty products that are just that. They have even gone a step further and pioneered the 'Quantitive Ingredient Listing' on all their products so that the consumer can clearly see what they are buying and therefore conduct their own research, and so avoid known irritants. Over a million people in the UK currently suffer from sensitivities caused by products used on the skin, which may vary from common allergies, sudden reactions and even disease.

The essential oils from citrus have their part to play in the cosmetics industry. This does not mean that if you use cosmetics made from citrus you will smell like discarded orange peel, far from it. The fragrances from the citrus essential oils are much sought after. It takes about one ton of the delicate white blossoms of the orange tree to make just one kilo of the essential oil.

'Prince of Neroli' is a range of products based on three of the citrus essential oils, namely Neroli, from the flowers, Petitgrain from the leaves and twigs, and Orange from the peel.

'Orange Bliss' is a beautifully fragrant hair and body wash which can also be used as a foaming bubble bath or a shower gel. It has a mild lather and gentle cleansing action.

A rich and creamy lotion 'Triple Orange Blossom Cream' is a fragrant solution to dry hands and feet as well as giving a velvet-smooth shave. This cream will help the razor glide over the skin without catching and can also be used immediately after shaving to make sure the skin keeps protected. Dry skin on the hands, body and feet will quickly absorb this rich moisturiser and used all over with the other products in the range will perfume the skin and brighten the day.

'Prince of Neroli Cologne' is a non-alcoholic body splash with the sensuous neroli fragrance. Added to the bath water this light and fragrant cologne 'deodorises the body, glorifies the bath and restores the spirit.' A little used to rinse through the hair after washing, and the hair will hold the freshness and fragrance all day.

174

The citrus ingredients in the cologne include: Lemon essential oil, stimulating, zesty and sharp; Orange essential oil from the orange peel, a warm round and fruity oil, also sharp and fragrant; Petitgrain essential oil, a favourite element in cologne blends; Orange flower oil, essentially the same as Neroli, but obtained in a slightly different way, and the Neroli essential oil itself, gentle for dry sensitive skin; stimulating healthy new cell growth; the bitter sweet fragrance lifts the spirits, soothes the nerves and acts as an aphrodisiac.

A by-product of the steam distillation of the flowers for the neroli oil, is Orange Flower Water. This is used in the product 'L'orange' a body shampoo for the shower, which will tone the skin. It is accompanied by double orange vinegar, which is used to balance the skin pH and for it's cleansing effect.

'Orange and Spice' is a 'whole orange' body soap with a clever blend of fragrances, and to make it a little bit special it is made to look like the real fruit, while tangerine essential oils are used with cocoa butter and white chocolate for a luxurious 'Tangerine Massage Bar' to help you loosen up in style.

The grapefruit is enormously refreshing and astringent when used as an ingredient in beauty products, and this effect is put to good use in the 'Freshly Squeezed Grapefruit Hair and Body Shampoo'.

It is a superbly energizing shower gel, suitable for daily use on the hair and body. It's stimulating 'wake up' power comes from real, liquidized grapefruit, that sharpens the senses and washes away weariness in an instant. It can be used as a shampoo as well, so your hair will also benefit.

'Whole Lemon Mask' is just what it says, the whole lemon is liquidised into a fresh citrus mask for it's astringent and toning properties, mixed with limeflower decoction, moisturising glycerine and deep cleansing kaolin and you have a refreshing, effective mask for normal to oily skins.

Lime flowers and walnut leaves boiled in water to produce a decoction are blended with henna and other ingredients to make natural hair colourants.

'Lemon Melt' is a thick gooey lemon scented shower jelly, containing Lemon juice concentrate, Lime essential oil, Orange essential oil and even a slice of lemon!

ORANGES IN INDUSTRY

We are all too familiar these days with tanker oil spillages on the high seas, particularly when it affects near-by land masses. The environmental clean-up operation often creates as much pollution as it is trying to resolve. This is because the detergents that are used in the process, dissolve in the water and spread. While the mess appears to be cleaned up, because seals and sea-birds no longer appear to be covered in oil, the detergent has actually sunk below the surface where it can cause long lasting damage by spreading through the food chain.

A new product produced from Oranges seems to be the solution. A small British company 'Pronatur Products', based in Bootle, has developed an orange based solvent which has the ability to separate oil and water, so that the oil can be collected easily. Tests have shown that it is non toxic to humans, animals, birds and marine life, and it has won the approval of the Ministry of Agriculture Fisheries and Food as well as the Department of Trade and Industry.

The product is called 'Pronatur Orange Solvent', a unique safe solvent cleaner and degreaser formulated from derivatives of orange oils and a synthesized mineral oil that catches fire only at high temperature (69°C/158°F) It replaces chlorinated and paraffin based solvents in most applications, thus offering a safer alternative for effective cleaning and degreasing. No special equipment, protective clothing, or ventilation is required, but for those with sensitive skins using the solvent for long periods, gloves are recommended as a precaution.

The product is particularly suitable for cleaning heavy crude oil spillages, like that of the *Exxon Valdez* but can also be used as a heavy duty domestic cleaner for removing mineral based problems such as tar, grease, carbon and bitumen. It will remove waxes, adhesives, uncured paint and varnish as well as oil based inks. 'Pronatur Orange Solvent' will also help clean up asphalt, creosote, chewing gum, silicon sealants and other mastics. It is ideal for cleaning oil spills off hard surfaces, cleaning combustion engines, parts washing, tank cleaning, electric motor cleaning and adhesive residue removal. Because 'Pronatur Orange Solvent' is completely non miscible with water, it is an ideal oily water separator. It is also available as a gel and as hand wipes.

'Pronatur Orange Solvent' is non-carcinogenic, non-aggressive and biodegradable, and where recovery is possible, it is 90% re-usable by volume.

COOKING WITH CITRUS

INTRODUCTION TO
COOKING WITH CITRUS

We have brought together many traditional and new recipes using citrus fruits for you to enjoy.

It is assumed that all fruit is washed before being used to remove any trace of fertilizer or pesticide. Fruit that is bought is often waxed, so use warm water to clean them and to dissolve the wax. Most citrus fruits yield greater quantities of juice if they are gently heated before juicing. This can be done by placing them in hot water for a few minutes or placing them into a microwave oven on defrost, for a few seconds.

The following conversion tables have been used and are intended as a guide and not an absolute. Please make any adjustment you may feel necessary.

$1/2$	oz	(15g)	$1/4$	pint	(150ml)
1	oz	(25g)	$1/2$	pint	(300ml)
2	oz	(50g)	$3/4$	pint	(450ml)
3	oz	(75g)	1	pint	(600ml)
4	oz	(100g)	$1 1/4$	pints	(750ml)
5	oz	(150g)	$1 1/2$	pints	(900ml)
6	oz	(175g)	$1 3/4$	pints	(1 litre)
7	oz	(200g)	2	pints	(1.2 litres)
8	oz	(225g)	$2 1/4$	pints	(1.35 litres)
9	oz	(250g)	$2 1/2$	pints	(1.5 litres)
10	oz	(275g			
11	oz	(300g)			
12	oz	(350g)			
13	oz	(375g)	$1/4$	tsp	(1.25ml)
14	oz	(400g)	$1/2$	tsp	(2.5ml)
15	oz	(425g)	1	tsp	(5ml)
1	lb	(450g)	1	tbsp	(15ml)
$1 1/4$	lb	(575g)	2	tbsp	(30ml)
$1 1/2$	lb	(675g)	3	tbsp	(45ml)
$1 3/4$	lb	(800g)	4	tbsp	(60ml)

150°C (300°F) gas mark 2   200°C (400°F) gas mark 6
175°C (325°F) gas mark 3   220°C (425°F) gas mark 7
180°C (350°F) gas mark 4   230°C (450°F) gas mark 8
190°C (375°F) gas mark 5

BUTTERS

DIPS

SAUCES

SOUPS

DRESSINGS

and

STARTERS

SAVOURY BUTTERS

LEMON AND BASIL BUTTER

Into 4 oz (100g) of butter, beat the finely grated peel of half a lemon 2 tsp (10ml) of lemon juice and chopped basil leaves to taste.

CORIANDER AND LIME BUTTER

Beat the finely grated peel of half a lime and 2 tsp (10ml) of lime juice with coriander leaves to taste, into 4 oz (100g) of butter.

ORANGE AND PARSLEY BUTTER

The finely grated peel of half an orange, 2 tsp (10ml) of orange juice and chopped parsley to taste, beaten into 4 oz (100g) of butter.

180

HUMMUS

Serves 8

2 14 oz (400g) tins chick peas
juice of 2 large lemons
1/4 pint (150ml) tahini paste
4 tbsp (60ml) olive oil
1-2 garlic cloves, skinned and crushed
salt and pepper
coriander leaves to decorate
serve with vegetable crudités

Place the drained chick peas in a food blender or processor, then gradually add the lemon juice to make a smooth purée.

Add the tahini paste, the oil, garlic and seasoning. Blend until smooth.

Spoon into a serving dish and decorate with coriander leaves. Serve with vegetable crudités.

BLUE CHEESE DIP

Serves 6-8

1/4 pint (150ml) soured cream
1 garlic clove, crushed
6 oz (175g) Blue Stilton cheese, crumbled
juice of 1 lemon
salt and pepper and snipped chives to garnish

Combine all the ingredients in a bowl and beat together well. Do not add too much salt as Stilton is salty. Put into a small dish and chill well. Garnish with snipped chives. Serve with savoury cocktail biscuits, stuffed olives etc.

COTTAGE CHEESE DIP

Serves 6-8

1/4 pint (150ml) soured cream
4 oz (100g) cottage cheese
juice of 1 lemon
salt and pepper
snipped chives to garnish

Combine all the ingredients in a bowl and beat together well. Put into a small dish and chill. Garnish with snipped chives. Serve with savoury cocktail biscuits, stuffed olives etc.

AIOLI DIP

Makes 1/2 pint (300ml)

4 garlic cloves, skinned
1/4 tsp (1.25ml) salt
2 egg yolks
1/2 pint (300ml) olive oil
2 tbsp (30ml) lemon juice

In a bowl, crush the garlic cloves with a little of the salt until a smooth paste is formed. Add the egg yolks and remaining salt and beat well. Gradually beat in the oil, a little at a time, until the mixture is thick and smooth. When all the oil has been added, beat in the remaining lemon juice. Store for up to 3 days in a screw-topped jar in the refrigerator.

GUACAMOLE

2 ripe avocados
1 beef tomato
1 small onion
juice of 1 lime
1 green chilli
tortilla chips to serve

Peel and mash the avocado. Finely chop the onion, tomato and green chilli and mix with the avocado adding the lime juice.

Serve at once with the tortilla chips.

CRANBERRY AND ORANGE SAUCE

8 oz (225g) cranberries
8 oz (225g) sugar
finely grated rind and juice of one orange

Put the cranberries in a pan and cover with $1/2$ pint (300ml) water. bring slowly to the boil and simmer for approximately 10 minutes until the cranberries have burst.

Add the sugar, the peel and the juice of the orange. Cook gently until the sugar has dissolved.

The sauce can be puréed for a smoother texture if preferred.

Serve cold with turkey or chicken.

Guacamole served with tortilla chips and Mexican beer

*Cranberry and Orange Sauce
served with a selection of cold meats*

184

CARROT AND ORANGE SOUP

Serves 6

1 oz (25g) butter or margarine
1 1/2 lb (675g) carrots, peeled and sliced
2 medium onions, skinned and sliced
2 pints (1.2 litres) Chicken stock
Salt and Pepper
1 medium orange
2 tbsp (30ml) cream
fresh coriander

Melt the butter in a saucepan, add the carrots and onions and cook gently until the vegetables begin to soften. Add the stock, season with salt and pepper and bring to the boil. Reduce the heat, cover and simmer for about 40 minutes, until the vegetables are tender.

Purée in a blender. Finely grate the rind from the orange and add to the soup. Squeeze the juice from the orange and add to the pan. Reheat gently and adjust seasoning. Garnish with a slice of orange cream and fresh coriander.

CREAM OF PUMPKIN AND LEMON SOUP

Serves 6

1 large onion, peeled and sliced
2 oz (50g) butter
1 lb (450g) pumpkin, peeled, seeded and cut into chunks
1/2 lb (225g) potatoes, peeled and sliced
1 small garlic clove, peeled and crushed
sprig of thyme
2 pints (1.2 litres) chicken stock (cubes)
salt
freshly ground black pepper
juice of 1 lemon
5 fl oz (150 ml) double cream

In a large heavy saucepan slowly cook the onion in the butter until soft and transparent.

Add the pumpkin, potatoes, garlic and thyme. Cover the pan and cook slowly for 20 minutes or until the vegetables are soft.

Add the stock with salt and pepper. Bring to the boil and simmer for 10 minutes. Remove the thyme sprig.

Purée the soup in a blender. Flavour it with lemon juice. Stir in the cream. Reheat without boiling.

CHESTNUT AND ORANGE SOUP

Serves 6

1 lb (450g) fresh whole chestnuts
1 1/2 oz (40g) butter or margarine
1 medium carrot, peeled and finely chopped
2 medium onions, skinned and finely chopped
4 oz (100g) wiped, and finely chopped mushrooms
1 tsp (5ml) flour
2 1/2 pints (1.5 litres) beef stock (cubes)
salt and pepper
1 tbsp (15ml) finely grated orange rind
chopped fresh parsley, to garnish

Split the brown outer skins of the chestnuts with a pair of scissors, or the tip of a sharp knife. Cook the chestnuts in boiling water for 3-5 minutes, drain and remove from saucepan. Peel off both the brown and inner skins and discard.

Melt the butter in a large saucepan, add the vegetables and fry together until lightly browned. Mix in the flour and cook, stirring continuously for a further 3-4 minutes, or until the flour begins to colour.

Off the heat, stir in stock, prepared chestnuts and seasoning. Bring slowly to the boil, stirring. Cover and simmer, for 40-45 minutes, or until the chestnuts are quite tender.

Purée the soup in a blender. Add half the orange rind and reheat to serve.

Adjust seasoning, add the remaining orange rind and garnish with the parsley.

TOMATO AND ORANGE SOUP

Serves 4

2 tbsp (30 ml) vegetable oil
1 finely chopped onion
2 garlic cloves, skinned and crushed
14 oz (400g) tin of chopped tomatoes
2 tbsp (30ml) tomato paste
1/2 pint (300ml) vegetable stock
1/2 pint (300ml) fresh orange juice
grated rind of 1 orange
1 tbsp (15ml) cornflour
2 tbsp (30ml) cream

Heat the oil and fry the onion and garlic until soft. Stir in the tomatoes, tomato paste, stock, orange juice and orange rind. Bring to the boil.

Combine the cornflour with a little water and stir into the soup until it thickens slightly. Add chopped fresh basil or dried basil and seasoning to taste. Serve garnished with a little grated orange rind and a swirl of cream.

CREAM OF LEMON SOUP

Serves 6

1 oz (25g) butter or margarine
2 onions, thinly sliced
3 oz (75g) carrot. thinly sliced
3 oz (75g) celery, thinly sliced
2 lemons
2 pints (1.2 litres) vegetable stock
1 bay leaf
salt and pepper
1/4 pint (150ml) single cream or Greek-style yoghurt
lemon slices, and celery leaves to garnish.

Melt the butter in a large saucepan and add the vegetables. Cover and cook gently for 10-15 minutes until the vegetables begin to soften.

Meanwhile, thinly pare the lemons using a potato peeler. Blanch the rinds in boiling water for 1 minute, then drain. Squeeze the juice from the lemons to give 5-6 tbsp (75-90ml).

Add the lemon rind and juice, stock and bay leaves to the pan. Season. Bring to the boil, cover and simmer for 40 minutes or until the carrots and celery are both very soft.

Cool soup a little, remove the bay leaf, then purée the the soup in a blender or food processor until quite smooth.

Return the soup to the pan, reheat gently, stirring in the cream or yoghurt. Do not boil. Adjust seasoning to taste.

Serve hot or chilled, garnished with lemon slices and celery leaves.

CURRIED PARSNIP AND ORANGE SOUP

Serves 4

2 oz (50g) butter or margarine
2 parsnips, diced
1 onion, chopped
1 garlic clove, crushed
1 tsp (5ml) curry powder
1/2 tsp (2.5ml) ground cumin
1/2 tsp (2.5ml) chilli powder
1 tbsp (15ml) flour
2 pints (1.2 litres) vegetable stock
finely grated rind and juice of 2 large oranges
salt and pepper
1/4 pint (150ml) single cream, to serve

Melt the butter in a large heavy-based saucepan. Add the parsnips and onion, cover the pan and fry gently for about 10 minutes until softened, shaking the pan frequently.

Add the garlic and spices and fry uncovered, for 2 minutes, stirring constantly to prevent burning. Stir in the flour and cook for a further 2 minutes, then pour in the stock and the orange juice. Bring to the boil, stirring, then add seasoning to taste. Lower the heat, cover and simmer for about 20 minutes until the parsnips are tender.

Mix the soup in a blender or food processor until smooth, then turn into a bowl, cover and leave overnight in a cool place or the refrigerator until cold, to allow the flavours to develop.

To serve, reheat the soup until bubbling, then lower the heat, stir in half the cream and heat through without boiling. Taste and adjust the seasoning.

Pour the hot soup into a warmed terrine or individual bowls, swirl with the remaining cream and sprinkle with the grated orange rind. Serve immediately.

PRAWN AND GRAPEFRUIT TARTLETS

Serves 4

4 oz (100g) filo pastry sheets, cut into 15cm (6 inch) squares
1/2 oz (15g) butter, melted
4 tbsp (60ml) mayonnaise
3 tbsp (45ml) fromage frais
1-2 tbsp (15-30ml) finely snipped chives
8 oz (225g) peeled prawns, thawed if frozen
1 pink grapefruit, peeled and segmented
thinly sliced radishes and cucumber, sprigs of fresh dill, to garnish

Arrange the filo squares at angles, in layers of four, brushing well with butter in between each sheet. (When cooked they will look like little fluted baskets).

Place in the lightly greased hollows of a shallow four-bun Yorkshire pudding tin. Bake in a preheated oven at 200°C (400°F) gas mark 6 for 5-6 minutes until just light golden brown. Remove from tin and cool.

Mix the mayonnaise, fromage frais and chives until well combined. Toss lightly with prawns and grapefruit segments. Spoon into prepared tartlets and garnish with radish and cucumber slices and sprigs of fresh dill. Serve immediately.

GRAPEFRUIT COCKTAIL

Serves 4

2 yellow grapefruits
2 pink grapefruits
1 tbsp (15ml) Crème de Menthe

Segment the grapefruits carefully removing all the white pith. Do this over a bowl to catch the juice. Place in the bowl.

Add the Crème de Menthe and stir to blend the flavour and colour. Leave to stand for 5 minutes.

Divide the segments between four cocktail glasses and spoon over the Crème de Menthe mixture.

HAZELNUT AND ORANGE DRESSING

Use to dress leaf or rice based salads

1 oz (25g) hazelnuts
1 oz (25g) butter
1 oz (25g) spring onions, trimmed and finely chopped
5 tbsp (75ml) dry red wine
2 tbsp (30ml) red wine vinegar
2 fl oz (50ml) hazelnut oil
2 oranges
4 whole green cardamoms
salt and pepper

Toast the hazelnuts under a hot grill for 3-4 minutes. Place in a tea towel and rub to remove the skins. Roughly chop.

Melt the butter in a small saucepan and sauté the spring onions with the hazelnuts until golden brown. Remove from the heat and add wine, wine vinegar, hazelnut oil, grated rind of 1 orange and 3 tbsp (45ml) orange juice.

Split the cardamoms and remove the seeds. Crush with a pestle and mortar. Stir into the dressing.

Peel the remaining orange with a sharp knife, removing all the peel and pith. Cut down between the membranes to release the orange segments. (Do this over the dressing to catch any juices). Stir into the dressing. Season to taste. Mix well before serving.

QUICK SALAD DRESSING

juice of half a lemon
1 tsp of salt (or to taste)
2 tbsp (30ml) of olive oil, walnut oil or groundnut oil

Mix well and pour over salad. Toss and serve.

QUICK TOMATO SALAD

Use the above mixture on thinly sliced tomatoes, with one small onion and a pinch of ground or fresh garlic.

MOZZARELLA ORANGE SALAD

Serves 4

2 oranges
2 beef tomatoes
2 mozzarella cheeses
1 tsp (5ml) olive oil
fresh basil and chives to garnish

Peel oranges and remove all white pith. Cut into slices

Slice tomatoes and cut mozzarella cheeses into slices.

MUSHROOMS IN LEMON CREAM

Serves 4

1 lb (450g) button mushrooms
juice of one lemon
2 tbsp (30ml) dry sherry
1/2 pint (300ml) cream
2 oz (50g) butter
2 oz (50g) parsley
slices of toast

Melt the butter in a frying pan. Wipe and quarter the mushrooms, and add to the butter. Cook until just turning colour. Add the lemon juice and sherry, bring to a fast simmer then stir in the cream. Continue cooking until thickened.

Place into warmed serving plate. Prepare heart shaped toast, dipped in sauce and sprinkled with parsley. Arrange on side of plate.

CEVICHE

Serves 6

1 1/2 lb (675g) fresh haddock fillets
1 tbsp (15ml) coriander seeds
1 tsp (5ml) black peppercorns
juice of 6 limes
juice of 1 orange
1 tsp (5ml) salt
1 hot red chilli (seeded and chopped)
4 tbsp (60ml) virgin olive oil
1 tsp (5ml) caster sugar
8 oz (225g) cucumber
2 small avocados
1 bunch spring onions, trimmed
few drops, up to 1 tsp (5ml) of Tabasco sauce (to taste)
3 tbsp (45ml) chopped fresh coriander
salt and pepper

Cut the haddock fillets either into small cubes or diagonal strips 1/2 inch (1.25cm) width and place in a bowl.

Crush the coriander seeds and black peppercorns to a fine powder and sieve to remove husks.

Mix with the juices from the fruits, salt, chilli, caster sugar and the olive oil. Pour over the fish, cover and place in the refrigerator for at least 12 hours (the longer the better), stir lightly from time to time.

The fish will become opaque. The lime juice has the effect of 'cooking' the fish.

To serve, drain the fish from the marinade, discarding the liquid. Thinly slice the cucumber. Halve, stone and peel the avocado and slice thickly. Shred the spring onions. Mix the cucumber, avocado and onions with the fish. Add the Tabasco sauce and fresh coriander and season to taste.

Serve chilled on a bed of shredded lettuce.

MACKEREL POTS

Serves 4

2 large cooked Mackerel fillets
4 large lemons
4 tbsp (60ml) mayonnaise
1/2 tsp (2.5ml) horseradish

Remove the tops of the lemons and save. Make a cut across the bottom of the lemon to secure a good base.

Hollow out the lemon by removing all the flesh from inside.

Skin and flake the mackerel, place the flakes in a bowl and combine with the mayonnaise, juice from 1 lemon and 1/2 tsp horseradish.

Generously refill the lemon pots using this mixture, loosely replace the lemon tops, garnish with chopped parsley and hot toast.

KING PRAWN
WITH LEMON AND TARRAGON
HOLLANDAISE

Serves 4

16 cooked king prawns
4 egg yolks
1/2 oz (15g) butter
1/2 tsp chopped parsley
1 tbsp (15ml) lemon juice
1 tbsp (15ml) wine vinegar
5 lemons
sprig of fresh tarragon

Arrange cooked prawns on a plate and garnish with lemon baskets and frisse lettuce. Heat lemon juice and wine vinegar (do not boil) and add to 4 egg yolks in a liquidizer. Blend for 10 seconds. Melt the butter on a low heat and pour slowly into the egg mixture with the liquidizer on full power. When fully combined pour into individual moulds and arrange on a plate and garnish with a sprig of fresh tarragon.

Mackerel Pots

King Prawn served with Lemon and Tarragon Hollandaise

DEEP FRIED CAMEMBERT
WITH CRANBERRY AND ORANGE SAUCE

Serves 4

8 wedges of Camembert
2 beaten eggs
4 oz (100g) bread crumbs
2 oz (50g) flour
$^1/_2$ pint (300ml) oil
4 oz (100g) cranberry sauce
1 pint (600ml) orange juice
2 oranges cut into wedges

Coat the Camembert with flour, beaten egg and bread crumbs, set aside and keep cool.

Place a frying pan on a medium heat, $^1/_3$ full of oil. When the oil is ready, place the wedges of Camembert in the oil and fry on each side until golden brown. Place on a warm plate.

Make the sauce by warming the cranberry sauce and orange juice together until it begins to thicken. Pour over the wedges of Camembert and garnish with orange slices and lollo rosso lettuce.

CHICORY AND CITRUS SALAD

Serves 4

1 small grapefruit
2 medium oranges
8 oz (225g) skinned tomatoes
2 chicory heads trimmed and washed
2 tbsp (30ml) sunflower oil
1 tbsp (15ml) lemon juice
2 tsp (10ml) caster sugar
3 tbsp (45ml) fresh parsley, chopped.

Segment the oranges and grapefruit discarding all the white pith and membrane. Do this over a bowl to catch the juice. Add the segments to the juice in the bowl.

Quarter the tomatoes and remove the seeds. Add to the bowl and mix with grapefruit and oranges.

Slice the chicory diagonally into $^1/_2$ inch (1cm) pieces. Open out the slices and add the tomato, grapefruit and orange mixture.

Place the oil, lemon juice, sugar seasoning and parsley into a bowl or screw top jar and whisk or shake well together. Pour over the chicory and fruit mixture and coat well. Adjust seasoning to taste. Cover and chill before serving.

AVOCADO CITRUS SALAD

Serves 4

2 large avocados
1 pink grapefruit
2 oranges
juice of 1 lemon

Halve the avocado with a sharp knife and remove stone. Carefully remove the skin. Slice lengthways thinly and arrange on a serving plate like a fan. Brush with lemon juice to avoid discolouration.

Arrange alternate slices of grapefruit and orange around the avocado. Garnish with a sprinkle of olive oil and chives.

MAIN COURSE DISHES

PERSIAN LAMB AND LIME CASSEROLE

Serves 6

2 lb (900g) lean stewing lamb washed and cut into large cubes
3 oz (75g) chick peas
3 oz (75g) black-eyed or butter beans
1 large onion, peeled and quartered
1 tsp (5ml) turmeric
salt and pepper
1 large or 2 medium potatoes, peeled and quartered
1 lb (450g) tomatoes, skinned and quartered
juice of 2-3 limes or lemons

Place the chick peas and the beans in a sieve and wash thoroughly under cold running water. Place in a bowl, cover with plenty of lukewarm water and leave to soak for at least 5 hours, preferably overnight. This helps them to cook evenly and in less time.

Put the meat in a large heavy saucepan. Cover with about 2 pints (1.2 litres) cold water and place over a moderate heat until the froth rises. Spoon off the froth and discard.

Drain the peas and beans and add to the pan with the onion, turmeric and pepper to taste.

Reduce the heat to a very low simmer, cover the pan and cook for 1-2 hours, until both meat and pulses are tender.

Add the potatoes, tomatoes and salt to taste, cover and simmer again for 10-15 minutes or until the potatoes are tender. Stir in the lime juice before serving. Serve hot.

LAMB CUTLETS WITH
ORANGE AND GINGER SAUCE

Serves 6

12 lamb cutlets
6 oz (175g) jar of stem ginger cut into match-sticks
2 oz (50g) butter
1/2 pint (300ml) orange juice
6 oranges
flour and seasoning
4 oz (100g) fresh parsley

Peel 4 of the oranges, cut into slices and quarter.

Melt the butter in a frying pan. Dust cutlets in seasoned flour and place in a pan with the butter. Cook slowly on a medium heat 5 minutes on each side. Remove from the pan and place on warmed serving dish and keep warm in the oven.

Add the orange juice and stem ginger with half it's juice to the pan, add the quartered orange segments and boil to reduce the liquid. Pour over the cutlets. Serve garnished with orange slices from the remaining oranges, and fresh parsley.

SUNSHINE CORNED BEEF

Serves 4

4 tbsp (60ml) olive oil
2 lb (900g) cold boiled potatoes, diced
1 large onion, peeled and sliced
salt and freshly ground black pepper
12 oz (350g) tin corned beef, diced
2 pink grapefruit, peeled and segmented
fresh chopped parsley, to garnish

Heat the oil in a large heavy based frying pan over a medium heat. Sauté the potatoes for 6-8 minutes, until just beginning to brown, stirring regularly. Add the onion and season well. Cook for a further 3-4 minutes until the onion softens. Stir the corned beef into the potato mixture and fry for 2-3 minutes.

Lightly toss the grapefruit segments with the cooked ingredients. Sprinkle with finely chopped parsley and serve immediately.

OXTAIL WITH ORANGE AND WALNUTS

Serves 4

1 large oxtail, lean or trimmed and jointed
1 oz (25g) flour
salt
freshly ground black pepper
4 tbsp (60ml) vegetable oil
2 onions, peeled and sliced
2 carrots, peeled and sliced
1/4 pint (150ml) beef stock (cube)
grated rind and juice of 2 oranges
1 bay leaf
2 oz (50g) chopped walnuts

Season the flour with salt and pepper and use to coat the oxtail. Melt the lard in a pan, brown the pieces of oxtail all over, then transfer to an oven-proof casserole. Brown the onions and carrots in the pan, then add to the casserole. Pour in the stock, then add the orange rind and juice, bay leaf, salt and pepper. Cover the casserole with the lid. Place in a preheated oven 150°C (300°F) gas mark 2 for 3^1/2-4 hours. Remove from the oven to a serving dish. Remove the bay leaf and sprinkle with the chopped walnuts.

BEEF AND LENTIL STEW WITH LIME

Serves 6

2 lb (900g) lean stewing beef, cubed.
4 oz (100g) lentils
3 oz (75g) black-eyed beans
1 tsp (5ml) turmeric
salt and pepper
1 small onion, peeled and quartered
1 medium uncooked beetroot, peeled and cut into ^{1}/2 inch (1cm) cubes
1 lb (450g) spinach leaves, washed and coarsely chopped
1 tsp (5ml) dried mint
juice of 4-5 limes or lemons

Put the lentils and the beans in a sieve and wash thoroughly under cold running water. Place in a bowl, cover with plenty of lukewarm water and leave to soak for at least 5 hours, preferably overnight. This helps them to cook evenly and in less time.

Put the meat in a large heavy saucepan. Cover with about 2 pints (1.2 litres) cold water and place over a moderate heat until the froth rises. Spoon off the froth and discard.

Drain the pulses and add to the pan with the turmeric and pepper to taste. Reduce the heat to the lowest possible simmer and add the onion and beetroot.

Cover the pan and cook for 1-2 hours, until both meat and pulses are tender.

Add the spinach, mint, lime juice and salt to taste. Cover and simmer again for a further 10 minutes. Serve hot.

STUFFED BREAST OF VEAL
WITH ORANGE

Serves 6

4-5 lb (2kg) breast of veal, boned
6 oz (175g) breadcrumbs
2 oz (50g) stoned raisins
2 oz (50g) currants
salt and black pepper
nutmeg
2 large oranges
The yolk from one large egg
2 oz (50g) lard
1 oz (25g) cornflour
caster sugar
6 tbsp (90ml) red wine

Prepare the stuffing by mixing the breadcrumbs, raisins, currants, a pinch of salt and pepper and nutmeg together in a bowl. Finely grate the rind from the oranges and add to the stuffing, together with the lightly beaten egg yolk. Stir in enough cold water to bind the mixture.

Spread the stuffing over the boned veal, roll it up and tie with thin string at 1 in intervals. Put the meat in a roasting tin. Add the lard and roast the meat for $2^{1}/2$ hours in the centre of a preheated oven at 200°C (400°F) gas mark 6 basting occasionally. Cover the meat with foil if it browns too quickly.

Put the meat on a serving dish but keep it hot in the oven. After removing the fat from the juices in the roasting tin, pour into a saucepan and heat. Blend the cornflour with 1 tbsp (15ml) of cold water and add to the juices, stirring continuously until the sauce has thickened. Bring to the boil and season to taste with salt, freshly ground pepper, sugar and nutmeg. Stir in the red wine and simmer the sauce gently.

Remove the white pith from the oranges and cut the flesh into small sections. Add these to the sauce and heat it.

Cut the veal into thick slices and arrange them on a warmed serving dish. Serve the sauce in a sauce-boat. Serve with orange and green salad, sauté potatoes and button onions.

VEAL WITH GRAPEFRUIT

Serves 6

3 lb (1.5kg) shoulder of veal
3 shallots, peeled and chopped
1 clove garlic, peeled and crushed
1 1/2 oz (40g) butter
2 tbsp (30ml) brandy
salt and pepper
3/4 pint (450ml) dry white wine
2 grapefruit

Trim and cut the veal into even pieces. Heat the butter in a saucepan and brown the veal pieces on all sides. Sprinkle with brandy and flame. Add the shallots, garlic, seasoning and wine. Lower the heat and cook for about 30-40 minutes.

Juice one grapefruit and segment the other, removing as much of the white pith and membrane as possible and saving all the juice. When the veal is cooked, pour the grapefruit juice into the pan and simmer for a further 5 minutes. Arrange the pieces of meat on a warmed serving dish, pour over the sauce and garnish with grapefruit segments slightly warmed in the oven.

LEMON PORK

Serves 6

2 lb (900g) boneless, lean pork
2 tbsp (30ml) flour
4 tbsp (60ml) vegetable oil
1 tbsp (15ml) grated green ginger
2 onions sliced
4 oz (100g) peeled and chopped tomatoes
2 tbsp (30ml) chopped parsley
juice of 2 lemons
1 pint (1.2 litre) chicken stock
2 tbsp (30ml) Greek yogurt
lemon wedges and chopped parsley to garnish

Cut meat into 1 inch (2.5cm) cubes and sprinkle with flour. Heat the oil and add the pork and ginger. Cook over a medium heat for a few minutes, turning occasionally. Add onions, tomatoes and parsley, cook for a few minutes more and add the lemon juice and stock.

Reduce heat and simmer slowly uncovered until the pork is tender and the stock is reduced. Just before serving stir in the Greek yogurt. Garnish with lemon wedges and chopped parsley.

CITRUS PORK

Serves 4

1 lb (450g) leg of pork, cut into $1/2$ inch (1.25 cm) pieces
1 oz (25g) butter
1 clove garlic, peeled and crushed
2 onions, peeled and chopped
Finely grated rind of 1 lemon
2 tbsp (30ml) lime juice
$1/4$ pint (150ml) vegetable stock (cube)
2 tbsp (30ml) single cream
1 egg yolk
salt and freshly ground black pepper
lemon and lime slices

Heat the butter, add the garlic and onions and fry for a few minutes, until transparent. Transfer to a small casserole dish.

Fry the pork for about 3 minutes, add to the casserole dish with grated lemon rind, lime juice and water, cook in the oven for about 40 minutes at 190°C (375°F) gas mark 5.

Place pork on a warmed dish. Mix the cream and the eggs, season well and pour in some of the lime juice mixture, beat well, add the remaining liquid, return to heat until sauce thickens. Taste and adjust seasoning. Garnish with slices of lime and lemon. Serve with creamed potatoes.

GRAPEFRUIT AND TARRAGON PORK

Serves 4

12 oz (350g) pork fillet, cut into $1/2$ inch (1.25cm) slices
5 tbsp (75ml) olive oil
4 tbsp (60ml) pink grapefruit juice
2 tbsp (30ml) fresh tarragon, finely chopped or
1 tsp (5ml) dried tarragon
salt and freshly ground black pepper
fresh vegetables in season

For the dressing:
3 tbsp (45ml) olive oil
2 tbsp (30ml) pink grapefruit juice
1 tsp (5ml) clear honey
2 tsp (10ml) fresh tarragon, finely chopped or
1 tsp (5ml) dried tarragon
salt and freshly ground black pepper
1 pink grapefruit, peeled and sliced

Place each piece of pork in between a folded piece of grease-proof paper and with a rolling pin or meat mallet pound until thin. Lay the pork in a shallow dish. Mix 4 tbsp (60ml) of the oil with the juice, tarragon and seasoning and pour over the pork. Cover and marinate for 1 hour in a refrigerator, turning occasionally.

In a mixing bowl or screw-top jar, make the dressing. Shake or mix the oil, juice, honey, tarragon and seasoning together. Remove the pork from the marinade and gently fry in the remaining oil until golden brown on each side.

Toss your choice of vegetables in the dressing. Arrange the pork and grapefruit into alternate slices in a fan shape, serve the vegetables and add more dressing to taste.

LIME PEPPERED CHICKEN

Serves 6

6 skinless chicken breast fillets
2 small yellow or red chillies, thinly sliced
2 tsp (10ml) black pepper
grated or shredded rind and juice of 3 limes
1 garlic clove, skinned and crushed
2 tbsp (30ml) clear honey
slices of courgette

Cut the chicken into bite-size pieces. Toss together the chicken, chillies, peppercorns, lime rind and juice, garlic and honey. Cover and marinate in the refrigerator for at least 30 minutes.

Thread alternate pieces of chicken and courgette onto metal or wooden skewers. Cook on the barbecue or under a grill for 10-12 minutes; turn frequently, basting with the marinade. Serve immediately with a Spicy Dipping Sauce of your choice.

BREAST OF DUCK
WITH ORANGE AND GRAND MARNIER

Serves 4

4 duck breasts
6 oranges
4 tbsp (60ml) oil
2 oz (50g) butter
4 tbsp (60ml) Grand Marnier

Trim 4 oranges and immerse in boiling water for about 20 seconds and drain. Juice these oranges.

Heat the oil to a medium heat in a pan. Dry the duck breasts with kitchen paper and place skin side down in the pan. Seal both sides. Place in a shallow oven proof dish and place in a pre-heated moderate oven 190°C (375°F) gas mark 5.

Drain the pan of oil and add orange juice and butter, boil for 2 minutes then add the Grand Marnier. Remove duck breasts from the oven. Place on a warm serving dish, slice if required and cover with sauce. Garnish with orange slices.

Lime Peppered Chicken

Breast of Duck with Orange and Grand Marnier

TURKEY AND ORANGE PARCELS

Serves 4

4 x 5 oz (150g) turkey steaks
4 rashers streaky bacon, with rind removed
4 spring onions, trimmed and chopped
1 oz (25g) breadcrumbs
1 orange, segmented
salt and freshly ground black pepper
2 tbsp (30ml) 'orange blossom' honey
4 tsp (20ml) sesame seeds

Grill or fry bacon until cooked through, chop and place in a small bowl. Place each turkey steak between 2 pieces of grease-proof paper and using a rolling pin or meat mallet, pound until thin.

To the chopped bacon, add spring onions, breadcrumbs and half the orange segments, roughly chopped. Season with salt and pepper. Divide stuffing into 4 and place in the centre of each turkey steak. Fold up to form small parcels and place on a baking tray.

Brush each parcel with honey and sprinkle over sesame seeds. Cook at 190°C (375°F) gas mark 5, for 25 minutes. Serve garnished with remaining orange segments.

ITALIAN MARINADED TROUT

Serves 4

4 whole trout (cleaned)
1 small bulb of fennel, trimmed and finely sliced
2 tbsp (30ml) olive oil
2 tbsp (30ml) flour
1 onion, skinned and finely sliced
1/2 pint (300ml) dry white wine
finely grated rind and juice of 1 orange
salt and freshly ground pepper
orange slices and chopped fennel tops, to garnish

Heat the olive oil in a frying pan. Dip the trout in the flour and fry gently for 4 minutes on each side. With a fish slice transfer the fish to a shallow dish.

With a sharp knife, score the skin diagonally, being careful not to cut too deeply into the flesh. Set aside.

Add the fennel and onion to the frying pan and fry for 5 minutes. Add the wine, orange rind and juice, and seasoning to taste. bring to the boil. Boil rapidly for 1 minute then add the chopped fennel tops and pour immediately over the fish. Leave to cool.

Marinate in the refrigerator for at least 8-24 hours.

Serve at room temperature garnished with orange slices and the chopped fennel tops.

SALMON STEAKS IN LIME

Serves 4

4 salmon steaks, about 6oz (175g) each
grated rind and juice of 4 limes
2 tbsp (30ml) chopped fresh basil
3 fl oz (75ml) dry white wine
4 garlic cloves, skinned and crushed
1 tsp (5ml) paprika
1 tbsp (15ml) sunflower oil
freshly ground black pepper
lime slices and chopped basil leaves to garnish

For the marinade, mix together the lime rind and juice, basil, white wine, garlic, paprika and oil in a non-metallic bowl, season to taste with black pepper.

Add the fish steaks and spoon over the marinade. Leave to marinate for at least 2 hours, carefully turning the fish at least once.

Remove the steaks from the marinade. Cook under the grill or on the barbecue for about 8 minutes on each side, basting with the marinade, until the fish is cooked through and the flesh flakes easily. Discard any remaining marinade. Serve immediately, garnished with the lime slices and chopped basil leaves.

MEDLEY OF COD, SUMMER VEGETABLES AND LIME IN A DRY WHITE SAUCE

Serves 4

1 lb (450g) cod fillet
6 oz (175g) young carrots
6 oz (175g) french beans
6 oz (175g) courgettes
1 glass dry white wine
1/2 pint (300ml) cream
2 oz (50g) butter
2 limes

Blanch all vegetables until 3/4 cooked and keep to one side.

Steam or poach the cod fillet, then flake. Melt the butter in a large frying pan adding the lime juice and wine. Add the cream, vegetables and fish flakes, bringing to the boil. Simmer until the mixture thickens to a good sauce texture.

Sprinkle with parsley and garnish with lime segments.

212

SEAFOOD PASTA

Serves 4

12 oz (350g) plaice
4 oz (100g) smoked mussels (tinned)
$1/2$ pint (300ml) cream
12 oz (350g) tagliatelle
Juice of 1 lemon
glass of dry white wine
1 oz (25g) butter

Cook and drain the tagliatelle in advance, set aside and keep warm.
Poach the plaice and flake the flesh onto a warm plate. Add to the liquid
the cream and, bring to the boil and continue boiling until it starts to
thicken. Add the tagliatelle, drained mussels, flakes of plaice and lemon
juice. Place a knob of butter into the sauce and gently stir.

Serve on a warm plate and garnish with chopped parsley.

213

BAKED MACKEREL WITH
ORANGE AND LEMON STUFFING

Serves 4

4 medium prepared mackerel (slit open and all bones removed)
$1/2$ oz (15g) butter
1 small onion, peeled and finely chopped
2 oz (50g) breadcrumbs
2 oranges, peeled, segmented and chopped
grated rind of 1 lemon
2 tbsp (30ml) lemon juice
2 tbsp (30ml) fresh parsley, chopped
salt and freshly ground black pepper

Melt the butter and fry the onion gently for 4-5 minutes until softened. Combine the remaining ingredients in a bowl, add the onions and mix. Divide the stuffing between the fish and wrap each in foil to form an open parcel. Place in an oven-proof dish and bake in the oven 190°C (375°F) gas mark 5, for 30-35 minutes. Serve with a crisp green salad and jacket potatoes.

MONKFISH WITH LIME AND PRAWNS

Serves 4

$1^1/4$ lb (575g) monkfish fillets, skinned boned, cut into 2 inch (5cm) pieces
2 tbsp (30ml) seasoned flour
2 tbsp (30ml) olive oil
1 small onion, skinned and chopped
1 garlic clove, skinned and chopped
2 tsp (10ml) chopped parsley
8 oz (225g) tomatoes, skinned and chopped
$1/4$ pint (150 ml) dry white wine
grated rind and juice of 1 lime
salt and pepper
4 oz (100g) cooked peeled prawns
lime slices, and fresh parsley to garnish

Coat fish in the flour. Heat the oil add the onion and garlic, fry gently until golden. Stir in the tomatoes, wine, seasoning, lime rind and juice. Bring to the boil. Place in a casserole dish. Cover and cook at 180°C (350°F) gas mark 4, for 15 minutes. Add the prawns and continue cooking until monkfish is tender. Serve garnished with lime slices and fresh parsley.

214

Desserts Cakes And Biscuits

CITRUS FLAN

Serves 6

Pastry
5 oz (150g) plain flour, sifted
3 oz (75g) butter, cut into small chunks
2 oz (50g) caster sugar
2 egg yolks
Egg Custard Base
$^1/_2$ pint (300ml) milk
1 vanilla pod
$2^1/_2$ oz (65g) caster sugar
3 egg yolks
$^1/_4$ oz (10g) flour
$^1/_4$ oz (10g) cornflour
Filling
3 oranges, peeled and segmented
1 white grapefruit, peeled and segmented
1 pink grapefruit, peeled and segmented

Make the pastry case, placing all the pastry ingredients into a bowl and initially using a fork, mix well together. When the ingredients are properly mixed, turn onto a floured board and knead gently until smooth.

Use the dough to line a 8 inch (20 cm) fluted flan case. Prick the base and bake blind in a preheated oven for about 20 minutes at 180°C (350°F) gas mark 4, until lightly browned. Remove from the oven and allow to cool in the tin.

Meanwhile, make up the custard base. Bring the milk and vanilla pod gently to the boil in a heavy saucepan.

Cream the sugar and yolks in a mixing bowl until light and fluffy, then sift the flour and cornflour into this mixture and fold in gently.

Remove the vanilla pod from the milk, and pour it over the egg and flour mixture, whisking vigorously. Rinse the milk pan and strain in the custard mixture. Whisk over the heat until the mixture thickens. Allow to cool, then spread it over the pastry base.

Arrange the fruit segments overlapping on top of the custard.

216

Citrus Flan

CITRUS SOUFFLÉ

Serves 6-8

finely grated rind and juice of 1 lemon
finely grated rind and juice of 1 orange
juice of 1 grapefruit
3 tsp (15ml) gelatine
4 eggs, separated
4 oz (100g) caster sugar
10 fl oz (250ml) double cream
crushed sweet biscuits and crystalised oranges and lemons, to decorate.

Prepare a 6 inch (18cm) soufflé dish. Cut a double thickness of grease-proof paper, enough to go around the outside of the dish and 2-3 inches (5-7.5cm) deeper to form a collar. Secure around the outside.

Place the fruit juices and gelatine into a heat-proof bowl, stand the bowl over a saucepan of boiling water until the gelatine is dissolved. Remove from the water and set to cool for 45 minutes.

Put the fruit rinds, egg yolks and sugar in a large heat-proof bowl and stand over the pan of boiling water. Whisk until the mixture is thick and holds a ribbon trail. Remove from the pan and whisk in the gelatine liquid. Leave until it is beginning to set, whisking occasionally.

Whip the cream until it will stand in soft peaks. Whisk the egg whites until stiff. Fold the cream into soufflé, then the egg whites, until evenly blended. Pour the mixture into the prepared soufflé dish and level the surface. Chill in the refrigerator for at least 4 hours until set. Carefully remove the paper from the edge of the soufflé. Press the crushed biscuits around the exposed edge, then decorate the top with crystalised fruit. Serve chilled.

MANDARIN CREAM CROWDIE

Serves 4

12 oz (350g) fresh satsumas, mandarins or clementines, peeled and segmented
2 oz (50g) medium oatmeal
10 fl oz (300ml) double cream
4 tbsp (60ml) 'orange blossom' honey
3 tbsp (45ml) Grand Marnier, Cointreau, or Curacao

Place the oatmeal in a grill pan and toast until golden brown, turning occasionally with a spoon. Leave for 15 minutes until cool. Whip the cream until just standing in soft peaks, then stir in the honey, liqueur and cooled toasted oatmeal.

Reserve a few segments for decoration, then layer up the remaining fruit and fresh cream mixture in four tall glasses. Cover with cling film and refrigeration for at least 1 hour. Remove from the refrigerator 30 minutes before serving. Decorate each glass with the reserved fruit segments.

MANDARIN ICE CREAM

Serves 4

12 mandarins
4 oz (100g) caster sugar
1 pt (600ml) thick cream
brandy-snaps to accompany

If using the freezing compartment of a refrigerator, turn it down to it's lowest temperature (highest setting) about an hour before you start.

Using a very fine grater, grate the skin from 6 of the mandarins and stir it into the caster sugar to flavour. Put the flavoured sugar with half the cream, in a heat proof bowl stood in a pan of boiling water. Heat this mixture to just below boiling point, stirring until the sugar has dissolved. Remove the bowl from the pan and leave mixture to cool.

Meanwhile, squeeze the juice from the mandarins. When the cream is cold, strain the mandarin juice into it and stir well. Whip the remaining thick cream to soft peaks and fold it into the flavoured cream. Pour this into a shallow freezer-proof container, cover and freeze for 1 hour, or until it is firm to a depth of 1 inch (2.5cm) around the sides of the container. Beat the ice cream vigorously with a fork or wire whisk to break down the ice crystals, then cover and freeze again until it is completely firm. Remove the ice cream from the freezer and place into the refrigerator half an hour before serving to soften slightly. Serve the ice cream in individual glass dishes with brandy-snaps.

SATSUMA AND KIWI PAVLOVA

Serves 8-10

4 satsumas or mandarin oranges
4 kiwi fruit
4 egg whites
pinch of salt
10 oz (275g) caster sugar
1 tsp (5ml) vanilla flavouring
1¼ tsp (6.25ml) cornflour
few thin slices of stem ginger
4 tbsp (60ml) rum
2 tbsp (30ml) ginger wine or syrup from the stem ginger
1 pint (600ml) whipped double cream

Put the egg whites in a large bowl and whisk until stiff and standing in
peaks. Slowly add 4oz (100g) of the sugar, whisking until the meringue
is glossy. With a metal spoon, fold in another 4oz (100g) of the sugar
with the vanilla flavouring and cornflour.

Cut a 10 inch (25cm) circle of grease-proof paper, lightly oil it and place
onto a baking sheet.

Spoon the meringue into a large piping bag fitted with a large plain
nozzle. Pipe the meringue in a spiral, starting at the centre of the
marked circle and working outwards towards the edge.

Pipe a second layer of meringue on top of the outer edge of the circle, to
make a raised side wall. Bake in the oven at 150°C (300°F) gas mark 2
for 1 hour until crisp and dry. Slide a large carving knife or metal
spatula between the grease-proof paper and the base of the meringue
to loosen, then slide the meringue off the paper onto a wire rack. Leave
to cool.

For the topping. Peel the kiwi fruit and slice thinly. Peel the satsumas
and divide into segments. Put the stem ginger in a bowl with the
remaining sugar, the rum and ginger wine or syrup. Add the prepared
fruit and stir gently to mix.

Just before serving, transfer the cold pavlova to a large serving platter.
Spread the whipped double cream in the centre, then arrange the fruit
decoratively on top. Pour over any juices.

CLEMENTINES IN ORANGE LIQUEUR

Serves 4

8 clementines, peeled and pith removed
6 oz (175g) caster sugar
1 pint (600ml) water
2 tbsp (30ml) Cointreau, Grand Marnier, or Curacao

Place the sugar and water into a large pan, bring to the boil, stirring constantly until the sugar has dissolved.

Add the clementines, bring back to the boil, then simmer gently for about 10 minutes. Leave to cool in the liquid.

Remove the fruit, boil down the syrup until reduced to about 1/2 pint (300ml). Cool, then add the liqueur. Pour over the clementines.

CLEMENTINE BISCUITS WITH APRICOT SAUCE

Serves 6

Biscuits
3 oz (75g) plain flour
pinch of salt
2 egg whites, lightly whisked
3 oz (75g) icing sugar, sifted
$2^{1}/_{4}$ oz (60g) unsalted butted, melted
icing sugar, for dusting

Filling
6-9 clementines peeled and segmented
$2^{1}/_{2}$ fl oz (100ml) milk
$^{1}/_{2}$ tsp (2.5ml) cornflour
1 egg yolk
$^{3}/_{4}$-1 oz (20-25g) caster sugar
drop of vanilla essence
2 tsp (10ml) brandy
2 tbsp (30ml) ground almonds
$^{1}/_{4}$ pint (150ml) whipped double cream

Sauce
8 oz (225g) dried apricots, soaked overnight
2 oz (50g) sugar
squeeze lemon juice

To make the biscuits, mix flour, salt, egg whites and icing sugar together in a bowl. Stir in the melted butter. Spoon the mixture in 12 equal rounds, spaced a little way apart, on lined and greased baking sheets. Bake in the oven at 180°C (350°F) gas mark 4 for about 10 minutes until lightly golden. Leave to cool on a wire rack.

To make the filling, heat the milk to boiling point in a pan. Meanwhile blend the cornflour with the egg yolk, then add the hot milk to the mixture stirring constantly as you pour. Pour the mixture back into the saucepan and cook over a low heat, stirring, until the sauce thickens. Remove from the heat and stir in the sugar, vanilla, brandy and ground almonds. Cover and leave to cool. When cold, fold in the cream.

To make the sauce, dissolve the sugar in about 4 tbsp (60ml) of water in a pan. Add the drained apricots and lemon juice, then simmer until soft. Purée in a blender or food processor, then leave to cool. Chill. Place the 6 biscuits on individual plates. Cover with the filling, then top with the clementine segments. Place the remaining biscuits on top and dust with icing sugar. Pour the apricot sauce around the biscuits and serve.

LIME AND RASPBERRY TART

Serves 8

Pastry
4 oz (100g) unsalted butter, melted
8 oz (225g) plain flour
pinch of salt
2 oz (50g) caster sugar
2 large egg yolks

Sift the flour and sugar into a bowl, add a good pinch of salt, the egg yolks and mix. Pour on the melted butter and mix until it forms a ball. Put in a plastic bag and chill for an hour. Roll out the pastry and cover a 9 inch (23cm) loose bottomed flan tin and chill.

Filling
3 thinly sliced limes
8 oz (225g) raspberries
8 oz (225g) granulated sugar
8 oz (225g) full-fat soft white cheese
4 tbsp (60ml) single cream
3 oz (75g) caster sugar
juice and grated rind of 2 limes
2 large eggs - beaten

Put sliced limes in a saucepan, cover with water. Simmer for 20 minutes. Strain 5 fl oz (150ml) of liquid and remove slices. Put measured liquid back in saucepan add granulated sugar, boil for a couple of minutes until thickened. Replace limes, simmer for 5 minutes, then allow to cool.

Mix the cheese, cream and caster sugar, gradually add the lime juice, beaten eggs and lemon rind. Pour into a chilled pastry case.

Place on pre-heated baking sheet at 180°C (350°F) gas mark 4 for 25-30 minutes, until well browned. Allow to cool. Arrange the lime slices and raspberries on top, pour over syrup. Do Not refrigerate before serving.

LIME POSSET

Serves 4-6

finely grated rind and juice of 2 limes
1 pint (600ml) thick cream
5 fl oz (150ml) dry white wine
2-3 tbsp (30-45ml) sugar
3 egg whites
fresh lime slices to decorate

Add the grated lime rind to the cream in a large bowl and whisk until stiff peaks form. Stir in the dry white wine. Next whisk in the lime juice, little by little and add sugar to taste. The posset should not be too sweet.

Whisk the egg whites until they form stiff peaks. Fold this into the whipped cream mixture and then chill. When ready to serve, whisk the posset one more time and serve in individual glasses. Garnish with a twist of fresh lime slices.

KEY LIME PIE

Serves 6

5 oz (150g) digestive biscuits
2$^1/2$ oz (60g) butter
1 oz (25g) demerara sugar
2 eggs, separated
7 oz (200g) tin condensed milk
grated rind and juice of 2 limes

Place the biscuits in a plastic bag and roll with a rolling pin to make fine crumbs. Melt the butter in a saucepan, then add the biscuits and sugar stirring well together to ensure that the butter coats all the crumbs. Line a 9 inch (23cm) loose-bottomed flan tin with grease-proof paper and lightly oil. Place the mixture in the tin, pressing over the base and up the sides to form a shell.

Beat together the egg yolks and condensed milk. Add the grated rind and juice from the limes and stir until thick. Whisk the egg whites until stiff and fold into the lime mixture. Pour into the biscuit shell and bake in the oven to 180°C (350°F) gas mark 4, for 20 - 30 minutes until set and just beginning to colour at the edges.
Alternatively, use a pastry shell, that has been baked blind.

224

Lime Posset

GRAPEFRUIT JELLY

Serves 6

1/4 pint (150ml) water
2 oz (50g) caster sugar (or to taste)
2 sachets gelatine
1/4 pint (150ml) white wine
1/2 pint (300ml) freshly squeezed pink grapefruit juice
pink grapefruit segments, mint sprigs and a little grated chocolate to decorate

Place the water and sugar in a saucepan and gently heat until sugar has dissolved then add the gelatine and stir until completely dissolved. Leave to cool slightly.

Stir in the wine and grapefruit juice and pour into a lightly oiled 1 pint (600ml) jelly mould and leave in the refrigerator to set, preferably over night.

To turn out, dip the mould in a bowl of hot water for a few seconds only, place an inverted serving plate over the mould and invert both, give a firm shake to free the jelly. Decorate with grapefruit segments, mint and chocolate before serving.

FRESH ORANGE JELLY

Serves 4

5 large oranges
4 oz (100g) cube sugar
5 tsp (25ml) powdered gelatine
1 tbsp (15ml) Cointreau, Grand Marnier or Curacao
fresh orange slices to decorate

Chill a 1 pint (600ml) jelly mould in the refrigerator. Rub the sugar cubes over the orange skins to extract the essence from the zest and place the sugar in a heavy based saucepan. Add 3 1/2 fl oz (100ml) water and make a syrup by stirring over a low heat until the sugar is completely dissolved. Remove the saucepan from the heat and reserve.

Squeeze the juice from the oranges, strain and measure out and make up to 12 fl oz (350ml), with a little water if necessary.

Combine the orange juice and sugar syrup, pour into a jelly bag or muslin lined sieve and leave for about 30 minutes to drip through into clean bowl.

Sprinkle the gelatine over $3^1/2$ fl oz (100ml) water in a small, heavy based saucepan and leave to soak for 5 minutes. Dissolve the gelatine over a low heat. Remove the pan from the heat and pour the dissolved gelatine slowly onto the strained orange juice, stirring constantly. Stir in the liqueur.

Rinse out the chilled jelly mould with cold water and pour in the orange jelly. Cover and leave in the refrigerator overnight or until set firm.

To turn the jelly out, dip the mould in a bowl of hot water for a few seconds, then place a plate upside down on top of the mould. Hold the plate and mould firmly and invert, give a firm shake to loosen and remove the jelly from the mould.

Arrange the orange slices around the base of the jelly just before serving.

ORANGE AND LEMON FOOL

Serves 6

3 medium oranges
1 lemon
3 oz (75g) caster sugar
$1/2$ pint (300ml) double cream
1 egg white

Finely grate the rind from the oranges and lemon into a small basin. Add the juice from the fruit and the sugar. Stir to dissolve the sugar in the fruit juices Place the cream and the unbeaten egg white into a large mixing bowl and whisk until the mixture is thick and light. Using a metal spoon, fold in the orange and sugar liquid until it is mixed thoroughly. Pour into six individual glasses and chill for several hours which will thicken the mixture.

Serve with sponge fingers.

CHOCOLATE AND ORANGE
SPONGE CAKE

12 oz (350g) flour
1/4 tsp (1.25ml) salt
2 tsp (10ml) baking powder
4 eggs
6 oz (175g) caster sugar
4 oz (100g) melted butter
finely grated rind of 2 oranges
4 fl oz (125ml) orange juice
4 oz (100g) dark unsweetened chocolate
4 oz (100g) unsalted butter
12 oz (350g) icing sugar

Beat the eggs and sugar together in a mixing bowl until frothy. Then fold in the sieved flour, salt and baking powder. Gradually beat in the butter, orange rind and orange juice. Divide the cake mixture between two sandwich tins 8-9 inches (20-23cm), lined with grease-proof paper, greased and floured.

Bake in the oven for 20-25 minutes at 180°C (350°F) gas mark 4 or until the cakes spring back to the touch. Cool for 5 minutes in the tin, then tun out onto a wire rack to cool. Meanwhile, melt the chocolate in a bowl over boiling water. Cream the butter with half the icing sugar then beat in the melted chocolate and the cream. Gradually work in the rest of the icing sugar.

Sandwich the two cakes together with about one third of the butter cream and use the remainder to cover the top and sides of the cake, fluffing it up to form peaks.

CHOCOLATE ORANGE COOKIES

4 oz (100g) self raising flour
2 oz (50g) butter
2 1/2 oz (60g) caster sugar
2-4 oz (50-100g) chocolate chips
Finely grated rind and juice of 1 orange
egg yolk

Cream together the butter and the sugar until light and fluffy. Add the orange peel, orange juice and egg yolk and mix thoroughly.

Chocolate Orange Sponge Cake

Chocolate Orange Cookies

ORANGE SURPRISE

Serves 6

6 large oranges
10 fl oz (250ml) double cream
2 oz (50g) icing sugar
6 tbsp (90ml) chunky orange marmalade
6 tbsp (90ml) orange liqueur
Leaves from your orange tree to decorate

Cut a slice off the top of each orange and save. Scoop out all the flesh, pips and juice from the oranges, saving the pulp, (chopped into fine pieces) and discarding any pips.

Whip the cream with the icing sugar until it forms stiff peaks. Mix together the liqueur, chopped orange and the marmalade. Fold the mixture into the cream until evenly distributed.

Spoon the cream mixture into the orange shells, so that it protrudes over the top. Freeze for at least 4 hours, preferably overnight (to allow the flavours to develop). Serve straight from the freezer, decorate with the reserved orange lids and the orange tree leaves.

ICED ORANGE SABAYON

Serves 6

6 egg yolks
6 oz (175g) demerara sugar
6 tbsp (90ml) orange liqueur
juice of six oranges to make 7oz (200ml)
orange segments to decorate

Put the egg yolks and sugar in a bowl and beat together until pale and creamy. Stir in the liqueur and the orange juice.

Pour into a saucepan and stir over low heat until the mixture thickens and just coats the back of the spoon. DO NOT BOIL.

Pour into 6 individual soufflé dishes or ramekins and cool for at least 30 minutes. Freeze for 3-4 hours until firm.

Serve straight from the freezer, decorated with orange segments.

RHUBARB AND ORANGE CRUMBLE

Serves 8

Cake mix
finely grated rind of 1 orange
6 oz (175g) butter or margarine
4 oz (100g) caster sugar
4 oz (100g) self-raising flour
2 eggs, beaten

1¼ lb (575g) rhubarb cooked and sweetened to taste
1 orange, peeled and thinly sliced in rounds

Crumble mix
4 oz (100g) plain flour
2 tbsp (30ml) granulated sugar
½ tsp (2.5ml) ground cinnamon
chopped nuts and orange segments for decoration

Grease a 9 inch (23cm) oven-to-table deep sided dish.

To make the cake base, mix 4 oz (100g) of the butter, the caster sugar, self-raising flour, eggs and orange rind together until smooth. Spoon into the dish.

To prepare the crumble, rub the remaining butter into the flour, then stir in the granulated sugar and the cinnamon. Spoon the cooked rhubarb over the cake mixture, layer the rounds of orange and sprinkle the crumble mixture over the top.

Bake in the oven at 200°C (400°F) gas mark 6 for 45 minutes-1 hour or until firm to the touch and golden brown. Decorate with chopped nuts.

PRUNE AND PORT FOOL WITH ORANGE

4 oz (100g) stoned prunes soaked over night in cold water
2 oz (50g) caster sugar
4 tbsp (60ml) port
finely grated rind and juice of 1 medium orange
¼ pint (150ml) thick custard, cooled
5 fl oz (150ml) double cream
sweet biscuits.

Drain the prunes, then put in a saucepan with the sugar, port, orange rind and juice.

Simmer for about 15 minutes until soft. Leave to cool slightly, then purée in a blender or food processor. Leave to cool completely.

Fold the cooled custard into the puréed prunes. Whip the cream until it stands in soft peaks, then fold into the prune custard until evenly blended.

Divide the mixture between four individual glasses, chill in the refrigerator for about 2 hours until firm and serve with sweet biscuits.

APPLE AND ORANGE CARAMEL

Serves 4

4 dessert apples, peeled, cored and thickly sliced
3 large oranges
3 oz (75g) granulated sugar
1/2 pint (300ml) water
1/2 tsp (2.5ml) vanilla essence

Caramel topping
4 oz (100g) granulated sugar
1/4 pt (150 ml) water

Place the sugar in a pan over a low heat to dissolve, then boil rapidly for 1 minute. Add the apples and vanilla essence and simmer for about 5 minutes, until fruit is tender. Remove from heat and leave covered, until cold.

Using a potato peeler, remove the rind from 1 orange, (do not remove the pith) cut into thin strips and boil for 5 minutes. Drain well and reserve for decoration.

Remove the peel and pith from the remaining oranges and slice into rounds.

For the caramel, place the sugar and water in a saucepan on a low heat until the sugar dissolves. Then bring the mixture to the boil and boil rapidly until the mixture caramelises. Pour onto an oiled baking tin and leave it to harden. Crack with a rolling pin.

Spoon the apples carefully into individual glass bowls with the syrup, arrange the orange slices on top and sprinkle the orange peel and cracked caramel pieces to decorate.

Serve chilled.

ORANGE LIQUEUR CREAM

1/2 pint (300 ml) carton double cream
1 tbsp (15ml) orange liqueur
2 tbsp (30ml) sifted icing sugar

Place the cream, orange liqueur and icing sugar in a bowl and whisk until soft peaks form.

Chocolate Orange Profiteroles

CHOCOLATE ORANGE PROFITEROLES

Makes 20 profiteroles

2¹/2 oz (65g) plain flour
pinch of salt
¹/2 pint (300ml) water
4 oz (100g) butter
2 size 3 eggs
¹/2 pint (300ml) whipped cream
Finely grated rind and juice of 1 orange
8 oz (225g) good quality chocolate
2 oz (50g) caster sugar

Sift the flour and salt onto a large plate.

Place the water and butter into a saucepan and heat slowly until the butter melts. Bring to the boil then lower the heat. Add the flour all in one go and beat until it has all been thoroughly mixed. Continue beating until the mixture forms a ball.

Remove from the heat and gradually beat in the eggs. The pastry should be smooth, shiny and firm, enough to hold soft peaks.

Spoon or pipe the mixture onto a greased baking tray, making approximately 20 small mounds.

Bake in a hot oven 220°C (425°F) gas mark 7 for about 25 minutes or until golden and well risen. Remove from the oven and immediately make a small slit in each to allow the steam to escape. Leave to go cold.

Meanwhile, melt the chocolate with the finely grated rind and juice of ¹/2 the orange, mix well. Dip the tops of the profiteroles in this mixture and allow to set.

Whip the cream with the caster sugar and the remaining juice (reserve the remaining finely grated rind) of the orange and pipe into each profiterole.

Serve with the remaining hot chocolate sauce and decorate with the finely chopped orange peel.

ORANGE MOUSSE

Serves 4

1/2 oz (15g) gelatine
3 eggs separated
3 oz (75g) caster sugar
2 large oranges

Dissolve the gelatine in a little boiling water and leave to cool. In a basin beat together the egg yolks and sugar until very light and creamy. Add the finely grated rind of one orange taking care not to grate in any of the pith. Squeeze juice from both oranges. Add to the mixture with the dissolved gelatine and mix well. Leave until it begins to set. Whisk the egg whites until they are stiff and forming peaks, then fold into the mixture. Pour into individual glasses. Chill for several hours before serving.

CHOCOLATE ORANGE

Serves 4

1 lb (450g) plain dark dessert chocolate
finely grated rind of 1 orange
juice of 3 oranges
2 oz (50g) butter
2 tbsp (30ml) Grand Marnier or Cognac .
4 egg yolks
2 egg whites
For decoration
1 orange
2 tbsp (30ml) Grand Marnier or Cognac

Break the chocolate and melt with the orange juice, finely grated rind and butter in a bowl over a pan of boiling water. Then remove it from the heat and stir in the 2 tbsp (30ml) of liqueur. Seperate the eggs, and whisk the yolks completely into the cholcolate mixture. Allow the mixture to cool. Whisk the egg whites until they will just hold peaks. Using a spatula, gently but thoroughly fold the whisked whites into the chocolate mixture. Pour the mixture into 4 individual 4 fl oz (150ml) glass dishes, cover and chill in the refrigerator for about 2 hours until they are set. Decorate with thin circular slices of orange cut into quarters. Pour 1 tsp (5ml) of Grand Marnier or Cognac over the top of each serving. Serve immediately.

CHOCOLATE ORANGE MOUSSE

Serves 4-6

4 oz (100g) dark eating chocolate
3 eggs
3 oz (75g) softened butter
1 oz (25g) castor sugar
grated rind of half an orange
1 tbsp (15ml) orange juice

Break up the chocolate and melt with the orange juice and rind in a
bowl over a pan of boiling water. Separate the eggs and whisk the yolks
completely into the chocolate. Take off the heat and whisk in the butter.
Leave until cool. Whisk the egg whites until forming peaks, then whisk
in the sugar. Fold into the chocolate mixture. Turn into a bowl or
individual dishes and chill for several hours overnight preferred, before
decorating and serving.

ORANGE CUSTARD CREAM

4 egg yolks
6 oz (175g) castor sugar
2 oz (50g) cornflour
2 tsp (10ml) grated orange rind
1 pint (1.2 litre) milk
1/2 pint (300ml) whipped double cream
1 tbsp (15ml) orange liqueur
2 tbsp (30ml) sifted icing sugar

Beat egg yolks and sugar in small bowl with electric mixer until pale and thick, beat in cornflour and orange rind, then gradually add milk, beat until smooth. Pour mixture into pan, stir constantly over heat until mixture boils and thickens. Cool to lukewarm, fold in cream, orange liqueur and icing sugar.

SAUCY LEMON PUDDING

Serves 4

When this pudding is cooked it separates into a light sponge top and tangy sauce underneath.

2 oz (50g) butter
6 oz (175g) caster sugar
1 large lemon
2 oz (50g) plain flour
1/2 pint (300ml) milk
2 eggs, separated

Cream together the butter and sugar until light and fluffy. Add the grated rind and juice of the lemon then mix in the flour and milk and beat in the beaten yolks. Fold in stiffly beaten egg whites and pour the mixture into greased dish.

Stand pudding dish in a baking tin filled with an inch of water and cook in a pre-heated, oven 190°C (375°F) gas mark 5 for 30-40 minutes.

The lemon sauce will separate out to be at the bottom of the pudding.

Serve hot.

LEMON-LIME ICED CREAM

Serves 6

3 eggs, separated
4 oz (100g) caster sugar
grated rind of 1 lemon
grated rind of 1 lime
2 tbsp (30ml) lemon juice
2 tbsp (30ml) lime juice
5 fl oz (150ml) whipped double cream
brandy snaps

Whisk the egg yolks and half the caster sugar until thick and pale in colour.

Stir in the grated rind and the juices of the lemon and lime. With a large metal spoon, fold in the whipped double cream.

Whisk the egg whites until stiff peaks form. Slowly add the remaining caster sugar and whisk until stiff and glossy. Fold this into the prepared mixture with a large metal spoon, lightly but thoroughly. Pour the lemon-lime cream into a 3 pint (1.8 litre) loaf tin or a freezer-proof container and freeze for 4 hours, or until firm.

To serve, divide the iced cream onto 6 individual glass dishes. Serve with brandy snaps.

RHUBARB AND LEMON FLAN

Serves 4-6

1 lb (450g) rhubarb, cut into 1 inch (2.5cm) lengths
grated rind of 1 lemon
juice of 1 lemon made up to $1/4$ pint (150 ml) with water
6 oz (175g) plain flour, sifted
3 oz (75g) white cooking fat or lard
2-3 tbsp (30-45ml) water
1 egg
6 oz (175g) soft brown sugar
1 oz (25g) cornflour
1 oz (25g) butter

Put the flour into a bowl and rub in the fat until the mixture resembles breadcrumbs. Add the water and mix to a soft dough. Chill for 30 minutes.

Roll out the pastry and line a 10 inch (25cm) flan tin. Arrange the rhubarb in circles in the flan tin.

Put the egg, sugar, cornflour, butter, lemon rind, lemon juice and water in a pan. Bring to the boil slowly, stirring all the time. Spread the lemon mixture over the rhubarb. Place in a preheated oven for 30 minutes at 180°C (350°F) gas mark 4, then increase the heat for a further 15 minutes to 200°C (400°F) gas mark 6. Serve warm

LEMON AND ALMOND TART

Pastry
4 oz (100g) plain flour
2 tbsp (30ml) castor sugar
2$^1/_2$ oz (65g) butter
2 egg yolks
1 tbsp (15ml) water
Lemon butter
2 oz (50g) butter
3 oz (75g) sugar
juice and finely grated rind of one large lemon
2 egg yolks
Filling
4 oz (100g) butter
1 tsp (15ml) vanilla essence
4 oz (100g) castor sugar
5 oz (150g) ground almonds
2 eggs, lightly beaten

Pastry
Sift the flour into a bowl, add sugar and rub in the butter. Add the egg yolks and enough water to mix to a firm dough. Roll out the pastry to line a greased 9 inch (23cm) flan tin. Prick the base all over with a fork, and bake blind in the oven 190°C (375°F) gas mark 5 for 15 minutes, and then allow to cool slightly. Spread lemon butter evenly over the base then pour on the filling. Bake in a moderate oven for 30 minutes or until set. Cool, decorate with whipped cream and toasted flaked almonds.

Lemon butter

Combine butter, sugar, lemon juice and egg yolks in a heat-proof bowl and stir over simmering water until mixture thickens slightly. Allow to cool.

Filling

Cream the butter, vanilla and sugar in small bowl until light and fluffy. Fold in the almonds and the eggs.

GLAZED LEMON TART

Serves 6

4 oz shortcrust pastry
1 tbsp (15g) plain flour
2 oz (50g) ground almonds
2 oz (50g) unsalted butter
2 oz (50g) caster sugar
1 egg
Rind of a lemon

Topping

2 small lemons
1 vanilla pod
8 oz (225g) caster sugar

Cut the lemons into thin rounds. Remove the pips and put the slices in a saucepan and cover with cold water. Bring briskly to the boil. Lower the heat, cover the pan and simmer gently for 1 hour or until the lemon slices are soft. Remove from the heat and let the slices cool in the liquid.

Roll the shortcrust pastry out on a lightly floured surface, to a circle of 9 inches (23cm). Grease a 7-8 inch (18-20cm) flan tin and line with the pastry. Prick the base lightly with a fork. Bake the pastry blind for 5 minutes, 190°C (375°F) gas mark 5.

Mix the flour and ground almonds. Beat the butter and sugar until soft and light. Beat the egg lightly and blend in the finely grated lemon rind. Gradually stir the egg into the butter mixture, then add the flour and ground almonds. Spread this mixture evenly over the pastry base. Place the tart just above the centre of the oven at 190°C (375°F) gas mark 5 and bake for 25-30 minutes or until the tart has risen and is golden brown and firm to the touch. Remove from the oven and leave to cool.

Drain the liquid from the lemon slices, setting aside $1/2$ pint (300ml). Add the vanilla pod and the sugar to the lemon liquid and cook in a saucepan over low heat until the sugar has dissolved. Add the lemon slices and simmer gently for about 5 minutes, then carefully lift the soft lemon slices on to a plate. Continue to boil the syrup rapidly until the mixture sets. It should coat the back of a spoon. Arrange the lemon slices in a circular pattern over the tart. When the syrup is setting, remove the pan off the heat, remove the vanilla pod, and as soon as the bubbles have subsided, spoon all the syrup over the lemon slices.

Leave the tart to chill on the refrigerator before serving it cold, cut into wedges.

LEMON CRUMB FREEZE

Serves 8

4 oz (100g) sweet biscuits crushed
2 oz (50g) castor sugar
2 oz (50g) butter
2 eggs, separated
1 small tin condensed milk
$1/4$ pt (150ml) double cream
finely grated rind and juice of 2 lemons
1 oz (25g) castor sugar

Melt the butter in a pan over a low heat. Place the biscuit crumbs in a medium sized bowl and add the sugar. Using a fork, stir in the melted butter until all the crumbs are coated. Reserving 2 tablespoons of the crumb mixture for the top, line the base of a freezer proof dish, which has been previously lined with a strip of grease-proof paper. Set aside to chill while preparing the filling.

Whisk together the egg yolks, condensed milk and cream. Add the lemon rind and strained juice and continue whisking until thickened.

Beat the egg whites until stiff and forming peaks and fold in the sugar. Fold gently into the lemon mixture and pour over the base of crumbs. Sprinkle the reserved crumb over the lemon mixture and freeze for 2-3 hours until firm. To serve, loosen the sides, lift out the dessert and cut in slices.

LEMON AND BLACKCURRANT FLUFF

Serves 4

Half of 5 oz (150g) tablet of lemon flavoured jelly
$2^1/_2$ fl oz (100ml) boiling water
$^1/_4$ tsp (1.25ml) finely grated lemon rind
1 tbsp (15ml) lemon juice
1 egg white
4 oz (100g) fresh blackcurrants (trimmed and washed)
$1^1/_2$ tsp (7.5ml) cornflour
2 tbsp (30ml) cold water
few drops of vanilla essence
sugar to taste (for the blackcurrants)

Dissolve the lemon jelly in a large bowl with the boiling water. Make up to 8 fl oz (250ml) with cold water. Stir in the lemon rind and juice. Chill until almost set. Add the egg white to the jelly mixture and whisk until light and fluffy. Pour into a mould or 4 ramekin dishes and chill until firm.

Meanwhile place the blackcurrants in a saucepan. Blend together the cornflour and cold water and add to the blackcurrants. Add sugar to taste. Cook over a medium heat, stirring constantly, until the mixture is thick and bubbly. Remove from heat and stir in the vanilla essence. To serve, un-mould the lemon fluff into a dish and spoon over the sauce.

LEMON SOUFFLÉ PANCAKES
WITH RASPBERRY SAUCE

Serves 4

Pancakes
2 oz (50g) plain flour, sifted
1 egg, beaten
$^1/_3$ pt (200ml) milk
lard, for greasing
Lemon soufflé filling
1 oz (25g) butter
1 oz (25g) plain flour
$^1/_2$ pint (300ml) milk
1 oz (25g) caster sugar

grated rind and juice of 1 lemon
2 eggs, separated
1 egg white
1 oz (25g) icing sugar
Sauce
8 oz (225g) raspberries
2 oz (50g) icing sugar
juice of 1 lemon

Put the flour into a mixing bowl, beat in the egg and milk to make a thin batter. Grease a 6 inch (15cm) frying pan and make 8 small pancakes, then set aside.

To make the filling, melt the butter in a pan, stir in the flour and cook for 2-3 minutes. Stir in the milk, sugar, lemon rind and juice. Bring to the boil, stirring well, then cook for 2-3 minutes. Cool slightly, then beat in the egg yolks.

Whisk the egg whites until stiff, then lightly fold into the mixture.

Put 1 tbsp (15ml) of the lemon mixture into each pancake, then fold it over. Sift a little icing sugar over each. Place in the oven 150°C (300°F) gas mark 2 for 10-15 minutes. Serve hot.

To make the sauce, sieve the raspberries into a bowl, then add the icing sugar and lemon juice and mix well.

HOT LEMON SOUFFLÉ

Serves 4

3-4 lemons
3 eggs, separated
4 tbsp (60ml) icing sugar
2 tbsp (30ml) flour
8 fl oz (225ml) milk
1 egg white
a little butter and sugar

Grease a 2 pint (1.2 litre) soufflé dish with the butter (include the rim) then dust with the sugar and shake out any excess. Finely grate the rind from one lemon and squeeze the juice from all the lemons to give 2 fl oz (50ml) of lemon juice.

Place the egg yolks in a bowl, sift in the icing sugar and beat until smooth, then add the sifted flour, continue mixing until quite smooth.

Bring the milk to the boil and then add to the mixture, whisking continuously.

Place the mixture in the milk pan and return to the heat, stirring constantly until the mixture thickens to a smooth custard. Add the lemon juice and grated rind and cook for a further 1-2 minutes, then pour the sauce into a mixing bowl.

Place the egg-whites into a bowl and whisk until stiff but not dry. Then quickly and evenly, fold the egg whites into the lemon custard.

Spoon the mixture into the prepared soufflé dish and smooth the top. Bake in the oven 200°C (400°F) gas mark 6 for 12-15 minutes until well puffed and golden. Serve immediately.

LEMON AND STRAWBERRY CHEESECAKE

Serves 6

3 lemons
8 oz (225g) strawberries
1 tbsp (15ml) strawberry jam
6 oz (175g) crushed digestive biscuits
3 oz (75g) melted butter
1 tbsp (15ml) powdered gelatine
8 oz (225g) low-fat soft cheese
1/2 pint (300ml) double cream
2 egg whites
a little cornflour to thicken
crystallized lemon jelly slices to decorate

Mix the crushed biscuits and melted butter together. With the back of a metal spoon, press the mixture over the base of a greased 8 inch (20cm) cake tin lined with grease-proof paper. Chill in the refrigerator to set whilst making the filling.

Finely grate the rind of 2 lemons and set aside. Squeeze the juice from the 2 lemons and make up to 1/4 pint (150ml) with water. Pour into a heat-proof bowl.

Sprinkle the gelatine over the lemon juice and leave to stand for 5 minutes until soft. Place the bowl over a saucepan of boiling water until the gelatine has dissolved. Remove the bowl from the water and set aside to cool slightly.

Whisk the cheese, and cream together in a separate bowl. Stir in the grated lemon rind and cooled gelatine and mix well.

Whisk the egg whites until standing in stiff peaks. Fold into the cheesecake mixture until evenly incorporated.

Spoon the mixture into the prepared base and level the surface. Chill in the refrigerator for at least 4 hours until set.

Wash and hull the strawberries reserving a few for decoration. put into a pan with the jam, stir until the jam has melted and thicken with a little cornflour. When cold, spread over the cheesecake and decorate with cream rosettes, the reserved strawberry quarters and the lemon jelly slices.

Lemon and Strawberry Cheesecake

Sift the flour and fold into the mixture. Stir in the chocolate chips.

Using a desert spoon, place portions of mixture 2 inches apart on a greased baking tray. Bake in the oven at 180°C (350°F) gas mark 4 for 15 minutes. Place on a wire rack to cool.

LEMON BISCUITS

4 oz plain flour and a pinch of salt
1$\frac{1}{2}$ oz (40g) butter
juice and grated rind of 1 lemon
1 egg yolk
2 oz caster sugar
lemon curd

Sift the flour and rub in the butter until it resembles fine breadcrumbs. Stir in the sugar and add the rind and juice of the lemon. Add the egg yolk and knead together to form a ball. Wrap in cling film and rest in the refrigerator for 40 minutes. Roll out and cut into rounds. Brush with milk and bake in the oven at 180°C (350°F) gas mark 4 for about 15 minutes until golden.

When cold sandwich together with lemon curd.

MIXED CITRUS CAKE

6 oz (175g) softened butter
6 oz (175g) caster sugar
3 standard eggs
8 oz (225g) plain flour, sifted
2 tbsp (30ml) milk
1$\frac{1}{2}$ tsp (7.5ml) baking powder
finely grated rind of 1 lemon, 1 orange, 1 satsuma or clementine

Prepare 8 in (20cm) cake tin (grease and line whole tin).

Cream the butter with the sugar, and citrus fruit rind thoroughly for 3-4 minutes until light and fluffy, adding 1 tbsp (15ml) of flour. Using a metal spoon, gently fold in the rest of the flour sieved together with the baking powder. Transfer to prepared tin and smooth the top with a knife. Bake for 1 hr 45 minutes in a the oven 175°C (325°F) gas mark 3. Leave in the tin for 5 minutes and then turn on to wire cooling rack.

CITRUS PRESERVES

SEVILLE ORANGE MARMALADE

2 lb (1 kg) Seville oranges
1 lemon
4 pints (2.4 litres) water
4 lb (2 kg) preserving sugar

Cut the fruit in half and squeeze out the juice. Remove the pips and tie in a muslin bag. Finely shred the fruit peel, put it into a large pan with the juice, water and muslin bag. Bring to the boil, then simmer for about 1 1/2 hours, until the peel is soft and the liquid reduced to about half.

Remove the muslin bag, and squeeze out any liquid from it.

Add the sugar to the pan and stir well until completely dissolved. Bring to the boil and continue boiling until setting point is reached.

The marmalade is ready when it coats the back of a spoon or creases when placed on a cold plate and pushed with the back of the finger.

Put the marmalade into sterilized jars, cover with waxed discs and when cold seal well with cellophane covers.

LIME AND TANGERINE MARMALADE

9 tangerines
3 limes
2 1/2 pints (1.5 litres) water
1 1/2 lb (675g) preserving sugar

Squeeze the juice from the tangerines and limes, and then shred the rinds of both as thinly as possible.

Put the juice, rind and the water into a saucepan, bring to the boil and simmer gently for 50 minutes, or until the rind is quite soft.

Add the sugar, boil for 5 minutes, and then test for setting.

Put the marmalade into sterilized jars, cover with waxed discs and when cold seal well with cellophane covers.

Preserves and juice for the breakfast table

ORANGE AND LEMON CURD

grated rind and juice of 2 large oranges
juice of half a lemon
8 oz (225g) caster sugar
4 oz (100g) butter
3 egg yolks

Place all the ingredients in a basin standing in boiling water. Mix well and continue to stir until all the sugar has dissolved.

Continue heating and stirring until mixture thickens enough to coat the back of a spoon, about 20 minutes. Do not allow the mixture to boil.

Pour into 3 sterilized jam jars, place a wax disc on top. When cold, cover with a lid or a cling film top. Store in the refrigerator.

GRAPEFRUIT AND LEMON MARMALADE

2 grapefruits
4 lemons
4 pints (2.4 litres) water
3 lb (1.3 kg) preserving sugar

Cut the grapefruits and lemons in half. Squeeze out the juice and strain into a preserving pan. Remove any membranes and pips and tie in a piece of muslin and put them in the pan with the water. Cut the peel into fine strips and add to the pan.

Boil until the shreds are tender and the contents of the pan reduced by almost half.

Remove the muslin bag, add the sugar and stir while the mixture is coming to the boil. Boil fast for 10 minutes, then test for setting.

Put the marmalade into sterilized jars, cover with waxed discs and when cold, seal well with cellophane covers.

LEMON AND LIME CURD

finely grated rind and juice of 3 lemons
finely grated rind and juice of 2 limes
8 oz (225g) butter
1 lb (450g) caster sugar
5 large eggs

Place all the ingredients in a basin standing in boiling water. Mix well and continue to stir until all the sugar has dissolved.

Continue heating and stirring until mixture thickens enough to coat the back of a spoon, about 20 minutes. Do not allow the mixture to boil.

Pour into sterilized jam jars, place a wax disc on top. When cold, cover with a lid or a cling film top. Store in the refrigerator.

Refreshing Citrus Drinks

LEMON SYRUP

2 pints (1.2 litres) of fresh lemon juice
3 lbs (1.3kg) of sugar
1 tbsp (15ml) of finely grated lemon rind

Put the juice, the sugar and rind into a saucepan. Heat slowly until the sugar dissolves, stirring constantly. Allow to simmer for 30 minutes.

Cool, then strain into sterilized bottles and seal.

Use 2 tbsp (30ml) of this syrup to each glass of water or soda-water. Store in a refrigerator.

FRESH LEMONADE

3 lemons
6 oz (175g) sugar (more or less according to taste)
1 1/2 pints (900ml) pints boiling water

Using a potato peeler, remove the rind from the lemons leaving the pith behind.

Put the rind and the sugar into a large jug and pour on the boiling water. Cover and leave to cool, but stir occasionally.

Juice the lemons and remove the pips. Add to the water. Strain and serve chilled.

SUNSHINE SODA

juice of one orange
1 tbsp (15ml) ice cream
1/2 glass of soda water

Whisk all the ingredients together in a blender until mixed and frothy.

Pour into a large glass and serve immediately.

Suggestions. Grapefruit, lime or lemon juice or any combination can be used.

ORANGE AND BANANA YOGURT DRINK

1 small peeled banana
juice of one orange
4 oz (150ml) natural yogurt
1 egg yolk

Whisk all the ingredients in a blender or food processor until it becomes a smooth mixture. Pour into a tall glass and serve immediately.

FRUITY CITRUS DRINK

juice from 2 pink grapefruit
juice from 1 lemon
1 egg
2 tsp (10ml) 'orange blossom' honey

Whisk all the ingredients in the blender or food processor until smooth. Adjust sweetness to taste using extra honey.

Pour into a tall glass and serve immediately.

CITRUS PUNCH

]juice of 2 grapefruits
juice of 2 lemons
juice of 5 oranges
$1/4$ pint (150ml) pineapple juice
$1^3/4$ pints (1 litre) soda water
sugar to taste
slices of lemon

Put all the ingredients into a punch bowl stir to dissolve the sugar. Refrigerate until served. Stir again and decorate with the lemon slices.

Limes can be used in place of lemon, if preferred.

Bibliography used for reference on Vitamin C.

1 American Journal of Clinical Nutrition. Spp to Volume 54 (no6). Dec 1991
2 Barker B M and Bender D A Vitamins in Medicine. Vol 2.
  William Heinemann. 4th Edition. 1982. pp1-68 and pp 291-318.
3 Cameron E and Pauling L. The orthomelecular treatment of cancer: The role of ascorbic acid in host resistance. Chem-Biol. Interact 9. pp 273-283   (1974).
4 Lind J A treatise on the scurvy. 1757.
5 Pauling L. Evolution and the need for Vitamin C. Proc. Nat. Acad. Sci. USA. 67. 1643-1648 (1970).
6 Pauling L. Vitamin C and the common cold. Freeman San Francisco (1970)
7 Pauling L. A re-evaluation of Vitamin C. Int. J Vit. Nutr. Res 47 (supp16), pp 9-17   1977
8 Szent-Gyorgyi A Lost in the twentieth century. Ann. Rev. Piochem. 32. 1976.pp 29-35.
9 Vitale J.J. Vitamins. 1st edition. Upjohn. 1976 pp 29-35.

'The Story of Honey' by Nestlés UK Ltd

If you plan to visit any of the Orangeries mentioned in this book, please check opening days and times before setting out on your journey.

For further information on products mentioned in this book, the following telephone numbers may be useful.

Trafalgar Home Improvements Ltd.		0703-263333
Pot Potential		0235-820930
Hare Lane Pottery		0725-517700
Ceramic Waterfalls		0227-722324
Biological Pest Control (Scarletts)		0206-240466
Cosmetics to Go	Freephone	0800-373366
Pronatur		051-9332282

For Information on the price and availability of Citrus Trees and the current price of our fertilizer, please send a stamped addressed envelope to:
Global Orange Groves UK, P.O.Box 644, Poole, Dorset. BH17 9YB.

We exhibit our trees at many flower shows during the summer season, including the Hampton Court Flower Show. Our Nursery is open any weekend we are not exhibiting. Our telephone number has an answerphone which will give the next opening date. We are always open over the Easter weekend. The Nursery is located at Horton Road, Horton Heath, Nr Wimborne, Dorset. BH21 7JN. Find Ringwood, Hampshire on the map, continue southward for a further 1/2 mile, turn right at the Ashley Heath roundabout (Horton Road) and continue for 5.5 miles.